First published in Great Britain 2016 by Red Shed,
an imprint of Egmont UK Limited
The Yellow Building, 1 Nicholas Road, London W11 4AN

www.egmont.co.uk

Text and illustrations copyright © Egmont UK Limited 2016

ISBN 978 1 4052 8136 2

Cartographic consultancy by Lynn Neal.

A CIP catalogue record for this book is available from the British Library.

Stay safe online. Any website addresses listed in this book are correct at the time of going to print.
However, Egmont is not responsible for content hosted by third parties. Please be aware that online
content can be subject to change and websites can contain content that is unsuitable for children.
We advise that all children are supervised when using the internet.

MIX
Paper from
responsible sources
FSC® C018306

ATLAS
of ODDITIES

Discover the amazing and diverse world we live in

Clive Gifford

RED SHED

Tracy Worrall

CONTENTS

INTRODUCTION

Eat rotting seabirds in Greenland.

Drop in at the world's first UFO landing pad in Canada.

PACIFIC OCEAN

N O R T H
A M E R I C A

Earth is an incredible and varied planet, packed full with an astonishing array of people, places and creatures.

Living on the planet are more than 7 billion people, all with their own interests, traditions and ways of life. And the extraordinary scenery – from icy poles to scorching hot deserts, lush tropical rainforests, giant rocky caves and canyons, remarkable rivers, lakes and seas – also provides a home to a phenomenally wide range of different animals and plants.

This unbelievable around-the-world adventure will take you through all of the planet's continents and countries, and on the way you'll get to see just how diverse the world can be.

Discover more about the countries or regions, and get up close and personal with some of Earth's most mysterious and unusual creatures, places, objects and events.

ARE YOU READY TO SEE OUR AMAZING WORLD IN A WHOLE NEW LIGHT?

Discover incredible cowboy boots in Mexico.

ATLANTIC OCEAN

S O U T H
A M E R I C A

Surf a never-ending wave in South America.

ARCTIC OCEAN

Go to a cucumber
festival in Russia.

Visit Sweden's
Nose Museum.

E U R O P E   A S I A

Visit Russia's largest museum, which
is guarded by around 70 cats.

Get an upside-down trim
from a hairdresser performing
a headstand in China.

Attend a camel beauty
pageant in Abu Dhabi.

PACIFIC OCEAN

A F R I C A

Check out deer with
fangs in India.

INDIAN OCEAN

O C E A N I A

See wombats leave cube-shaped
poos in Australia.

Watch the world's fastest grape
tramplers at the Whoosh Festival
in South Africa.

Head to Antarctica to visit
a sculpture garden.

A N T A R C T I C A

ICELAND

EUROPE

ATLANTIC OCEAN

IRELAND

UNITED KINGDOM

NORTH SEA

NETHERLAND

BELGIUM

LUXEMBOURG

BAY OF BISCAY

FRANCE

SWITZERLA

ANDORRA

PORTUGAL

SPAIN

Covering just 1/50th of the Earth's surface, Europe may be the second smallest continent, but it is packed with incredible places and over 740 million people. Home to many amazing cultures and civilizations, such as the ancient Greeks and Romans, it is also the birthplace of industry and the location from which intrepid adventurers, including Columbus, Magellan and Captain Cook, set sail to explore the world. Europe's landscape is extremely varied, from the snowy mountains of the Alps mountain range and icy winter Baltic Sea coastlines to warm Mediterranean regions, rolling plains and many wooded areas, including the Black Forest in Germany.

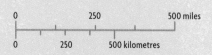

0	250	500 miles
0	250	500 kilometres

BARENTS SEA

NORWEGIAN
SEA

SWEDEN

NORWAY

FINLAND

RUSSIA
Sits in both
Europe and Asia

ESTONIA

LATVIA

DENMARK

BALTIC
SEA

LITHUANIA

KALININGRAD
Part of Russia

BELARUS

ERMANY

POLAND

CZECH
REPUBLIC

UKRAINE

ECHTENSTEIN

SLOVAKIA

AUSTRIA

HUNGARY

MOLDOVA

CASPIAN
SEA

SLOVENIA
CROATIA

ROMANIA

BOSNIA AND
HERZEGOVINA

SERBIA

BLACK SEA

MONTENEGRO

KOSOVO

BULGARIA

ITALY

MACEDONIA

ALBANIA

TURKEY
Sits in both
Europe and Asia

GREECE

MALTA

CYPRUS

MEDITERRANEAN SEA

BARENTS SEA

NORWEGIAN SEA

100 miles

0   50   100 miles

0   50   100 kilometres

EUROPE ASIA

AFRICA

FINLAND

5. ROVANIEMI
Over half a million letters addressed to Santa Claus from all over the world find their way to a special post office just north of this town, on the Arctic Circle.

5

4. OULU
This chilly city hosts the World Air Guitar Championship every year. Rock on!

4

Oulu has an average temperature of 2.7°C.

Torneälven river

The middle of lake Koltajärvi in Koltajärv (6) is a border between three countries: Finland, Sweden and Norway.

6

7

Mandeg

18. BODØ
Home of the Grandmothers Festival since 1992, where grannies bungee jump, motorcycle and scuba dive.

7. JUKKASJÄRVI
The Icehotel has been built here every year since 1990. It's created each time from a huge amount of snice (a mixture of snow and ice) – enough to make 700 million snowballs! Guests stay in icy rooms and even sleep on ice beds.

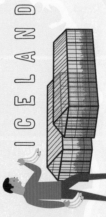

18

S W E D E N

NORWEGIAN SEA

ICELAND

Iceland is Europe's least densely populated nation. First settled by Viking explorers over 1,000 years ago, Iceland's 329,000 people are listed in the phone book by their first names.

100 miles

0   50   100 miles

0   50   100 kilometres

N

19. STRANDAGALDUR
The only known surviving pair of nábrók are at The Icelandic Sorcery and Witchcraft Museum. These trousers were made from the skin of a dead person and were once believed to improve the success of spells cast by sorcerers.

19

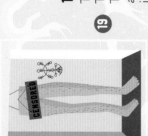

CENSORED

A school in Reykjavik, called Álfaskólinn, is devoted to the study of elves. Experts are sometimes called out in Iceland to advise whether a boulder can be moved or if it is an elf's home.

REYKJAVIK ★

20

I C E L A N D

20. HVERAGERÐI
A giant banana plantation is housed at Iceland's Agricultural University on top of an ancient lava field. The greenhouses are heated by geothermal energy from below the Earth's surface.

17. STATOIL TROLL A GAS RIG
A concert featuring Katie Melua and her band rocked out 303m below sea level at the Troll A gas rig, in a shaft at the bottom of the North Sea.

17

3. SONKAJARVI

The Wife-Carrying World Championships involves athletes racing around a course, each with a lady slung over their shoulder.

2. KUMMAKIVI

A giant rock balances precariously on another rock deep in a Finnish forest. Local legend says it was carried there by giant trolls, but scientists think that glaciers carried the rock instead.

Finland has a staggering 187,888 lakes. Lake Saimaa (1) is its biggest and the only home of the rare Saimaa ringed seals.

★ HELSINKI

Scandinavia has an area of over **1.2 MILLION KM²**, yet has a population of fewer than **27 MILLION**. Norway has over **1,150 FJORDS**. Finland has more than **179,000 ISLANDS**, while no one in Denmark is ever more than **52KM** from the sea.

BALTIC SEA

The 72m-high Telefonplan Tower in Stockholm features a large light display that can be controlled by anyone with a mobile phone and an app. Users can dial up and pick the lights' colours.

★ STOCKHOLM

GULF OF BOTHNIA

SCANDINAVIA

Scandinavia is the name given to the region of northern Europe that contains Denmark, Sweden and Norway, and together with Iceland and Finland they form the Nordic Countries. The terrain varies — from warm, lowland pastures in Denmark to rugged mountains in Sweden, Norway and Finland. Snow, ice and forests cover much of the northern parts that are inside the Arctic Circle.

8. BJURHOLM 🄈

The Elk House is the only farm in the world that produces moose cheese for sale.

Österdalälven river

9. LAKE MÄLAREN

A single room underwater hotel can be found in the middle of Lake Mälaren. The Utter Inn is only reachable by inflatable dingy.

Over 210 million IKEA catalogues are printed each year.

10. ÄLMHULT

One of Europe's largest photographic studios is found in this small town (8,000 population). It's responsible for taking all the photos of IKEA products for its catalogue.

11. LUND

The Nose Academy contains a large collection of plaster cast noses belonging to famous Scandinavians.

12. MALMÖ

A 6m-high talking lamp in Malmö gives Christmas greetings in Swedish during the Christmas season.

16. TRONDHEIM 🄰🄶

Lazy cyclists not fancying the steep climb up the city's Brubakken hill can use the CycloCable — the world's first bicycle lift on the road. Cyclists place one foot on a plate that pushes them up the hill.

14. AURLANDSFJORD

Perched on a steep side of a fjord, Stigen Gard was a farm where the only access was via a ladder. In the past, when officials came to collect taxes, the farm dwellers used to pull the ladder up!

Glomma river

LÆRDALS TUNNELEN 24.5KM

15. LAERDAL

At 24.5km long, the Laerdal tunnel is the world's longest road tunnel. In 2000, Vibeke Skjerping and Ronny Rinde had their wedding in the tunnel.

★ OSLO

13. DYREHAVSBAKKEN

Since 1957, hundreds of Santas have attended the World Santa Claus Congress each year. It's held at Dyrehavsbakken — the world's oldest amusement park.

D E N M A R K

🄭🄶 ★ **COPENHAGEN**

The Dyrehavsbakken amusement park first opened in 1583.

Sneezing powder was invented in Denmark by Søren Adam Sørensen!

NORTH SEA

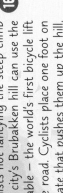

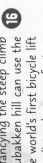
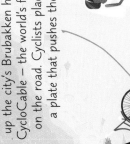

UK AND IRELAND

The UK is made up of Europe's largest island – Great Britain (England, Scotland and Wales) – and Northern Ireland, and is home to more than 64 million people. Over the years, people from the UK and Ireland have invented many things – from trains and the World Wide Web to the chocolate bar.

The UK has a **12,429KM-LONG COASTLINE** and with an area of **243,610KM²** is the **80TH LARGEST COUNTRY** in the world but the **22ND MOST POPULOUS**, with an estimated **64.5 MILLION INHABITANTS.** More than **ONE-EIGHTH** of Britons live in Greater London.

15. FOULA, SHETLAND ISLANDS 15

When Britain changed calendars from the Roman Julian calendar to the Gregorian calendar in 1752, the island of Foula did not. As a result, it now celebrates Christmas Day on the 6 January and New Year on the 13 January.

14. ORKNEY ISLANDS

The world's shortest scheduled commercial flight is between the two Orkney islands of Westray and Papa Westray. Operated by Loganair, the flight can last as little as 47 seconds.

In 2011, Scottish band, FOUND, released their new single 'Anti Climb Paint' on a record made of chocolate. The limited edition record could be played on a normal record player and the record sleeve was also edible as it was made of rice paper.

13. EGREMONT

A crab fair has been held in this village since 1287, but in more recent times it has been home to the World Gurning Championships. Contestants put their heads through a horse collar and pull a ridiculous face. The champion is the one who gains the most applause from the crowd

SHETLAND ISLANDS

ORKNEY ISLANDS 14

NORTH SEA

SCOTLAND

★ EDINBURGH

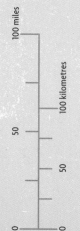

1. GIANT'S CAUSEWAY

Volcanic activity, about 50–60 million years ago, created this incredible collection of 40,000 interlocking hexagonal (six-sided) columns of basalt rock. According to Irish legend, the mythical giant, Finn McCool, used them as stepping stones to cross the sea to fight the Scottish giant, Benandonner.

ATLANTIC OCEAN

0   50   100 miles

0   50   100 kilometres

JANUARY

EUROPE
ASIA
AFRICA

NORTHERN IRELAND

★ BELFAST

ISLE OF MAN

DOUGLAS ★

IRISH SEA

★ DUBLIN

REPUBLIC OF IRELAND

CELTIC SEA

ENGLISH CHANNEL

11. COWLINGE

Jamie-Louisa Arnold, a 12-year-old girl, bit into an apple in 2002 to discover a gold ring inside. When newspapers ran the story, a lady recognized the ring as the one she had lost in a swimming pool in Essex 27 years earlier.

12. KNARESBOROUGH

First opened to the public in 1630, the well in this cave contains water so rich in minerals that objects left in it for months appear to turn to stone.

10. WILLASTON

A Worm Charming World Championships (urging worms out of the ground without digging them up) has taken place here since 1980.

LONDON

King Henry III (1207–1272) was given three lions, a polar bear and an elephant as gifts from other rulers during his reign.

ENGLAND

CARDIFF

W A L E S

9. LLANWRTYD WELLS

At the World Bog Snorkelling Championships, competitors swim their way through a muddy bog wearing flippers, a mask and a snorkel, in the shortest possible time.

8. PORT TALBOT

A museum devoted to baked beans opened here in 2009. The museum's curator, Barry Kirk, has changed his name to Captain Beany, eats beans with every meal and, at the museum, dresses up in an orange superhero suit. In 1986, Kirk sat in a bathtub full of baked beans for 100 hours.

6. STONEHENGE

In 1915, Stonehenge was sold at auction for £6,600 to lock-making millionaire Cecil Chubb. He bought it as a present for his wife but she didn't like it so he donated it to the nation in 1918.

7. MARGATE

A father and son were digging a duck pond in 1835 when they discovered 21m-long underground passageways lined with around 4.6 million seashells. No one knows who built the Shell Grotto or why!

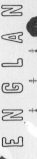

5. AXMINSTER

This is the birthplace of William Buckland, president of the Royal Geographic Society and the first man to publish a scientific study about dinosaurs. Buckland attempted to eat every single animal that existed as a meal – from panthers to porpoises.

2. LAMBAY ISLAND

This is populated by wild wallabies, relatives of the kangaroo that are normally found over 15,000km away in Australia. They were first released onto the island by Dublin Zoo in the 1980s.

In 2012, artist Frank Buckley built a home in Dublin out of 1.4 billion (£1 billion) worth of shredded Euro banknotes bundled into bricks.

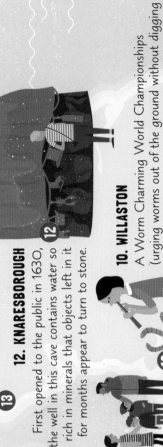

3. WATERVILLE

This small town erected a bronze statue of movie actor Charlie Chaplin in 1998, and since 2011 it has held a Chaplin film festival every year to commemorate the time he visited the town on holiday.

4. ISLES OF SCILLY

A Dutch admiral declared war on the Isles of Scilly in 1651, but the Netherlands forgot to declare peace and so the war technically lasted until 1986 when the two sides signed a peace treaty.

WESTERN EUROPE

Bordering the Atlantic Ocean to the west and the Mediterranean Sea to the south, western Europe consists of two tiny nations, Andorra and Monaco, dwarfed by three much larger countries, France, Spain and Portugal. Sailors from these last three countries explored much of the world and, at one time, Spain's empire covered almost one-fifth of the world's land.

A Z O R E S

1

The *Mary Celeste* was discovered drifting along the ocean near the Azores islands in 1872 with its cargo intact but no one onboard the ship! Investigations were held in Gibraltar, but no one was able to explain what had happened to the ship and its crew.

1. PONTA DELGADA

In 2012, 3,000 copies of the *Terra Nostra* newspaper went on sale. Not a big deal you would think, until you realize that it was the world's smallest newspaper, measuring 18mm x 25mm and weighing precisely one gram!

France is the most visited country in the world with **83.7 MILLION** arrivals in 2014. Spain is third with **65 MILLION** tourists. Portugal receives around **8.1 MILLION** visitors per year. Even the tiny territory of Andorra, with an area of **468KM²**, attracts over **2.3 MILLION** visitors each year.

2. FUNCHAL

Famous footballer Cristiano Ronaldo paid for a new museum to be built in Funchal, where he was born, that is all about himself. The CR7 Museum is dedicated to his life and houses most of his 140 awards.

M A D E I R A I S L A N D S

2

A T L A N T I C   O C E A N

5. PORTO

The São João festival starts every 23 June and involves people showing affection for one another by hitting each other on the head with soft plastic hammers.

5

6. JUNCAL DO CAMPO

This town has some of the oldest graffiti artists. A collection of graffiti-making grandmas are part of Lata 65, a group who spray-paint walls and buildings.

6

Schoolchildren on the island of La Gomera (3) are taught the Silbo Gomero language, which is thought to be over 400 years old. It is made up of whistling sounds that are used to communicate over long distances.

3

C A N A R Y I S L A N D S

4

4. LANZAROTE

The El Diablo Restaurant in Timanfaya National Park cooks food over a volcano. A hole bored into the dormant volcano releases over 400°C of heat for seriously scorching cooking.

P O R T U G A L

★ **LISBON**

Guadiana r

The Hospital de Bonecas, in Lisbon, has been looking after and repairing damaged dolls since 1830. People from all over the world send their dolls here to be 'operated' upon.

0	100	200 miles
0	100	200 kilometres

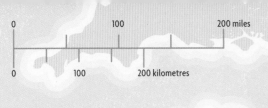

17. ALCOLEA DEL PINAR

[...]ino Bueno Utrilla spent [...]5 years, from 1907 onwards, [...]arving a seven-room home out of [...]ock using only a pickaxe. When he [...]nished it, the Spanish government [...]ere so impressed that they gave [...]im a medal and five acres of land.

16. NANTES

French students built a vehicle in 2014 that can travel over 3,200km on a single litre of fuel. The Microjoule weighs just 35kg and was the brainchild of students at La Joliverie College.

 16

Loire river

15. Y

 Y

The town with one of the shortest names in the world is also one of France's smallest towns, with fewer than 100 people living there.

15

★ PARIS

Seine river

Bacon perfume was invented in Paris by butcher John Fargginay, in 1920. The original recipe was then lost during the 1920s, but in 2011, the perfume went on sale again.

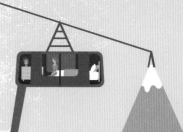

14. SOMMET DE LA SAULIRE

It is possible to stay the night in a cable car hanging over 2,700m above sea level near this mountain's summit.

F R A N C E

12. TRIE-SUR-BAÏSE

Hundreds of people dress up as pigs, attempt to make the most realistic pig noises and generally ham it up at a festival called La Pourcailhade.

13. VALENCE

Caterpillars were put on trial in 1535 for eating the crops of a local landowner. The caterpillars were sentenced by the judge to be banished from the local area!

14

MASSIF CENTRAL

Rhône river

13

ALPS

 NO LOCALS

CASINO

Only foreigners are allowed into Monaco's casinos. Citizens aren't allowed in unless they work there.

BAY OF BISCAY

12

PYRENEES

Garonne river

Andorra is ruled by two people, called co-princes, and neither of them live in the country. One co-prince is the President of France and the other is the Bishop of Urgell, a city in northern Spain.

★ MONACO

MONACO

9. EL VENDRELL

A public toilet for dogs was opened here in 2014. The stainless-steel doggy potty has a flushing lever and is connected to the towns' sewerage system.

ANDORRA

 ★ ANDORRA LA VELLA

CORSICA

Duero river

 S P A I N

17

8 9

10. BARCELONA

The Teatreneu comedy club started a Pay-Per-Laugh scheme in 2014. Facial recognition computer software registers each time someone laughs and charges per chuckle. So if you don't laugh at all, then you see the show for free.

★ MADRID

7. BUÑOL

Ever since the 1940s, the end of August has been marked in this Spanish town with a massive tomato fight, called La Tomatina, in the town square.

7

10

€

11

BALEARIC ISLANDS

11. MINORCA

In 2011, scientists discovered the fossil of a giant prehistoric rabbit on this island, that was more than six times the size of a modern bunny. *Nuralagus rex* may have weighed 12kg and had short legs so didn't hop around.

Over 150,000 tomatoes are squashed, hurled and splattered in two hours of tomato-ey mayhem.

8. TARRAGONA

Human towers up to nine people high, are formed by acrobats, known as castellers, at the Concurs de Castells competition each year. It takes them years of training.

MEDITERRANEAN SEA

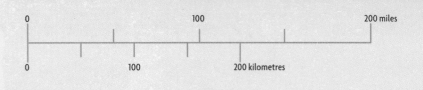

13. BAARLE (BAARLE-HERTOG AND BAARLE-NASSAU)

Although Baarle may look like one town, it is in fact two separate settlements with two fire brigades and two police forces. This is because the border between Belgium and the Netherlands runs through the middle of some streets and cafes, and even cuts through some houses so that the front door is in Belgium and the back door is in the Netherlands.

14. CULEMBORG

To slow down the speed of rush-hour traffic, this town's council released six sheep onto the streets in 1996. Sheep and cows also replaced the town's lawnmowers to keep the grass in public areas nice and short.

NETHERLANDS
★ AMSTERDAM

BELGIUM

★ BRUSSELS

12. STEKENE

Hotel CasAnus allows you to spend a night in a giant-sized part of the human digestive system, as it looks like a human colon.

15. WINTERBER

The first World Wok Racing Championshi took place here in 2003. Woks, which ar normally used for cooking, were sat in an raced down a fast, icy bobsled trac

11. WITTLICH

The Wittlich Fame Academy is for animals. Viviane Theby, an animal trainer, has managed to teach dogs to dance, a cat called Roti to play the piano, and even a chicken called Katie to play the xylophone!

★ LUXEMBOURG

LUXEMBOURG

G E R M A N

10. LUDWIGSHAFEN

King Bansah of the people of Hohoe, Ghana lives in this town and governs his 200,000 subjects in Africa using Skype and emails.

8. ESTAVAYER-LE-LAC

The Frog Museum contains 108 stuffed frogs posing like people. For example some are playing cards and others are sitting at the dinner table. They are the art of François Perrier, a guard who created them between 1848 and 1860.

9. REUTLINGEN

The world's narrowest street, called Spreuerhofstrasse, can be found in this historic market town. At its narrowest point, the street is just 31cm wide.

S W I T Z E R L A N D
★ BERN
VADUZ ★ LIECHTENSTEIN
ALPS

7. MOUNT NIESEN

There is a staircase on the side of this mountain that contains a leg-aching 11,674 steps. One day each year, the 3.4km-long staircase is opened to runners who attempt to get to the top in the quickest possible time.

6. BELALP

Every January about 1,500 skiers dress up as witches and race down the slopes using broomsticks instead of ski poles. The race began in 1983 and commemorates the days when a real witch was said to live close by.

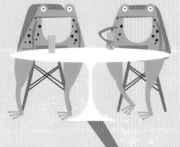

BALTIC SEA

The biggest country in western and central Europe is Germany (357,022km²). The smallest is Liechtenstein, which at 160km² is smaller than Washington DC in the USA. In the southern part of the region lies Europe's biggest mountain range, the Alps.

Elbe river

1. KRAUSNICK

The Tropical Islands Resort has sandy beaches and a warm temperature all year because it's housed in a giant aircraft hangar previously used for storing airships. It has a tropical rainforest containing 50,000 plants and a pool mimicking a coral reef.

★ BERLIN

An entire museum in Berlin is devoted to Germany's most popular street snack – the currywurst (a pork sausage covered in a spicy tomato sauce).

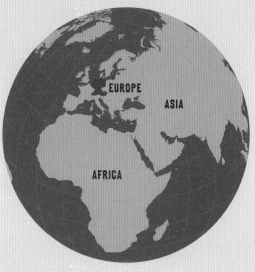

EUROPE
ASIA
AFRICA

2. SCHKEUDITZ

Planes taxi over car roads on special bridges between the runways of Leipzig/Halle Airport.

Some of Germany's odd laws include: it is illegal to not let a chimney sweep into your house if they ask, it is against the law to recycle your glass bottles at certain times of the day and it is also illegal to have your piano tuned at nighttime!

3. DARMSTADT

The Waldspirale apartment building in Darmstadt has 1,000 windows, none of which are the same design. The curving U-shaped building also has a roof covered in trees and grass.

The Alps stretch **1,200KM** across parts of **11 COUNTRIES** and contain **82** official mountain peaks that are over **4,000M** in height. The tallest of all is Mont Blanc at **4,810M HIGH**.

Danube river

5. LAUFEN

Regina Mayer trained a cow, called Luna, as a showjumper. Luna is able to leap over 1m-high barriers.

VIENNA ★

4. HERRNBAUMGARTEN

Sleeping bags for bats and mini guillotines for fingernails are among the many exhibits at Nonseum – a museum for ideas and inventions that nobody really needs.

A U S T R I A

The Vienna Vegetable Orchestra use about 70kg of fresh vegetables each time they play a concert. They carve the veg into musical instruments, such as pumpkin drums, leek violins, carrot flutes and red pepper trumpets.

Despite a total population of just 37,000 and measuring only 24.8km by 12.4km, Liechtenstein is the world's biggest manufacturer of false teeth, producing up to 60 million sets of gnashers every year.

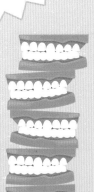

11. IVREA

Over half a million oranges are imported to this northern Italian city every year for a giant food fight! As many as 5,000 people splatter each other with this fruit to commemorate a rebellion against an evil baron who ruled the region centuries earlier.

12. GRAN PARADISO NATIONAL PARK

Wild alpine ibex goats climb the almost vertical slopes of 49m-high Cingino Dam in order to lick salt off its walls. They do this because they don't get enough of this mineral from their vegetarian diets.

13. ERACLEA

There is a ban on building sandcastle on the beaches here. You can be fine up to 250 Euros if you get out you bucket and spade and start digging

Po river

SLOVENIA

★ LJUBLJANA

★ ZAGREB

CROATIA

BOSNIA AND HERZEGOVINA

SARAJEVO ★

SAN MARINO

10. REGGIO

The Credito Emiliano bank's vaults hold hundreds of thousands of wheels of Parmesan cheese. The bank stores them as security on the bank loans that it gives to local cheese farmers.

14. PLJEŠEVICA

This large mountain hides a secret . . . an underground airport built in the 1960s to hold military jets and enough food and supplies for over 1,000 people to stay inside the mountain for at least 30 days.

ITALY

ROME ★

VATICAN CITY

Instructions on bank cash machines in Vatican City, the world's smallest country, are in Latin — the state's official language. 'Insert your card' is displayed as *Inserito scidulam*.

9. VACONE

You cannot get a more exclusive restaurant than Solo Per Due — it only has one table and two seats! There can be a waiting list of several years for this tiny diner.

★ TIRANA

ALBANIA

7. MOUNT ATHOS

Although technically part of Greece, Mount Athos is a monastic state that is run according to its own rules — women and female cows, sheep or goats aren't allowed here.

GREECE

★ ATHENS

SICILY

MEDITERRANEAN SEA

6. PHAISTOS

Found in 1908, the Phaistos Disc is a 10.5cm-wide clay disc dated at around 3,700 years old. It is covered in 45 different symbols, which scientists and archaeologists have yet to work out. Is it a prayer, a secret code or a disc used in printing? No one knows!

Many churches in Malta have two clocks on their walls, both of which show different times in order to confuse the devil.

MALTA ⑧ VALLETTA

CRETE

8. SPINOLA BAY

Gostra is a Maltese game played every August where men try to run up a 10m-long pole, covered in grease, to reach one of the three flags fitted to the top. The pole is perched over the water so competitors usually end up in the sea.

EASTERN MEDITERRANEAN

This region was home to a series of great civilizations and empires, including ancient Greece (c. 1200–323BCE), the Roman Empire (27BCE–474CE), the Byzantine Empire (395–1453) based in southeastern Europe, and the Ottoman Empire (c. 1300–1922), which had its centre in Turkey and also controlled territory in Europe and the Middle East. In 2006, two of Europe's newest nations were formed when Serbia and Montenegro split and became separate countries.

About **47.1%** of the land in Italy and **63.4%** of the land in Greece is used for farming. Turkey and Italy produce **90%** of the world's hazelnuts. Turkey also grows more than **11.8 MILLION TONNES** of tomatoes each year – the most in Europe.

0 — 100 — 200 miles

0 — 100 — 200 kilometres

1. KUSKÖY
People in this mountainous area use a 400-year-old language made up of different whistles, just like birds. The whistles of *kuşdili* (meaning bird language) travel further through the hills and valleys than shouting – as far as one kilometre.

BLACK SEA

2. SARICAYIR VALLEY
Climbers travel 1,800km inside a large cave in this valley to collect a special honey that is rich in minerals. This 'Elvish' honey sells for about £3,500 per kilogram – making it more valuable than gold.

T U R K E Y

In 1829, every man who worked for the government of the Turkish Ottoman Empire had to wear a fez hat by law. In 1925, the new ruler of Turkey, Mustafa Kemal Atatürk, banned the fez from being worn by anyone in the country.

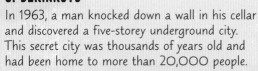

Tigres river

★ ANKARA

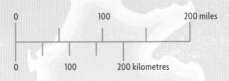

4. ÇEŞME
Mehmet Ali Gökçeoğlu replaced his home's front fence with a gigantic 50m-long aquarium that holds hundreds of fish, eels and even octopuses.

3. DERINKUYU
In 1963, a man knocked down a wall in his cellar and discovered a five-storey underground city. This secret city was thousands of years old and had been home to more than 20,000 people.

NICOSIA ★
C Y P R U S

Cyprus and Greece are the only nations in the world who share a national anthem. The Hymn to Liberty has a staggering 158 verses of words but a short version is usually played.

EUROPE

ASIA

AFRICA

5. CHIOS ISLAND
Every Easter Sunday for over 100 years, two churches that are 400m apart in the town of Vrodandos appear to go to war with each other. The churches fire about 60,000 rockets at their rival's church bell in a tradition known as Rouketopolemos (Rocket War). To protect the churches, they are boarded up and covered with metal sheets.

1. JELGAVA

Since 2002, a race has been held every August on the Lielupe river for boats made only out of thousands of empty milk cartons. The race is part of Latvia's Milk, Bread and Honey Festival.

TALLINN ★

BALTIC SEA

ESTONIA

⑬

RIGA ★

LATVIA

①

②

2. SAMOGITIA

Hidden underwater, secret stone roads (known as *kulgrindas*) allowed local people to escape invaders by providing safe walkways through marshes and swamps. Some were built on ice over 700 years ago, so when the ice melted, the roads became submerged under a shallow level of water.

LITHUANIA

VILNIUS ★

Twin brothers Remigijus and Egidijus Praspaliauskas from Vilnius, design and sell shoes over the internet that are made out of bread.

MINSK ★

P O L A N D

B E L A R U

A travel agency in Prague began offering holidays in 2010. However, Toy Traveling offers holidays only for people's cuddly toys. Each owner receives a daily email update from their toy and a photo album of it seeing the sights.

3. KUTNÁ HORA

Sedlec Ossuary is a small chapel decorated with the bones of more than 40,000 skeletons. Thousands of skulls and other bones have been used to make decorations, such as a chandelier and a coat of arms.

★ WARSAW

5. SZYMBARK

An upside-down house here took about five times longer to complete than a normal house because it made the builders feel dizzy and sick. Entry is through a roof window.

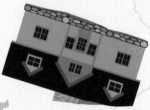

Vistula river
⑤

PRAGUE ★ ③

CZECH REPUBLIC

④

Vltava river

SLOVAKIA

⑫

Dniester river

★ BRATISLAVA

BUDAPEST ★

HUNGARY

⑩

4. BRNO

A 400m-long model train set runs through the Výtopna restaurant. It's used to deliver drinks to the restaurant's customers.

Over 400 supporters of Spanish club Atletico Bilbao travelled to Budapest in 2012 for the UEFA Europa League final, only to discover they had gone to the wrong capital city. The game was being played in Bucharest, Romania.

R O M A N I A

⑧

This region's longest river is the **2,850KM-LONG DANUBE** that starts in Germany but runs through eight countries in this region. In 2014, more than **100,000 SHIPS** travelled along the Danube, carrying **10.1 MILLION TONNES** of goods.

6. ZASAVICA SPECIAL NATURE RESERVE

The world's most expensive cheese comes from a group of donkeys at this nature reserve. Pule cheese is crumbly and white, and has a strong flavour. Less than 100kg is made each year.

⑥ ★ BELGRADE

BUCHAREST ★

Danube river

S E R B I A

Danube river

⑦

MONTENEGRO

PRISTINA ★

★ SOFIA

PODGORICA ★

KOSOVO

B U L G A R I A

★ SKOPJE

MACEDONIA

Pule cheese costs over £700 per kilogram.

13. OTEPÄÄ

The European Sauna Marathon is held here every winter. Competitors run through the snow between 20 different saunas and spend three minutes inside each sweltering hot cabin.

In Belarus' capital, Minsk, there has been a national mobile phone throwing competition every year since 2002. Events include longest throw and precision tossing into a plastic bucket. It's so popular that it is shown on TV.

KIEV ★  U K R A I N E

Dnieper river

BANG!

12. TERNOPIL

The first bulletproof vest was invented by a priest who was born in Ternopil. Kazimierz Zeglen tested it on himself in 1897 by donning the vest and getting a friend to fire five bullets at him. Fortunately, the vest was a success!

MOLDOVA

★ CHIŞINÂU

⑪

10. TRANSYLVANIA

Half a million pieces of Lego have been used to build a working, driveable car that runs on air. It was built by Raul Oaida, a self-taught Romanian engineer.

⑨

BLACK SEA

7. KALOFER

Every January, men in traditional costumes wade into the icy cold waters of Tundzha river and perform an ancient dance called the *Horo*.

Some trovants have a circular or oval pattern of rings inside, similar to tree trunks.

This region has been home to mighty empires — from the Romans to the Ottomans and Austro-Hungarians. Six of these countries (Moldova, Ukraine, Belarus, Latvia, Lithuania and Estonia) formed part of the former Soviet Union until 1991, while Macedonia, Serbia and Kosovo were once part of Yugoslavia. Until the 1st January 1993, Slovakia and the Czech Republic were one country — Czechoslovakia.

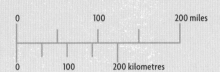

11. MILESTII MICI

The two villages that make up Milestii Mici have a secret below ground. They are home to the world's biggest wine cellar, which contains 200km of tunnels and holds about 1.5 million bottles of wine.

9. MISKHOR

Ukraine has an underwater painting school on the shores of the Black Sea. The artists are trained scuba divers and have just 40 minutes of air in their tanks to dive underwater and paint. They have special canvasses covered with an adhesive waterproof coating to which their oil colours stick.

8. COSTESTI

This area of Romania is famous for having trovants — rocks that grow in size. They have a stone core and an outer shell of stone. When it rains heavily, minerals in the rain combine with chemicals in the stone and cause small stone-like forms to appear on their surface.

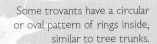

23

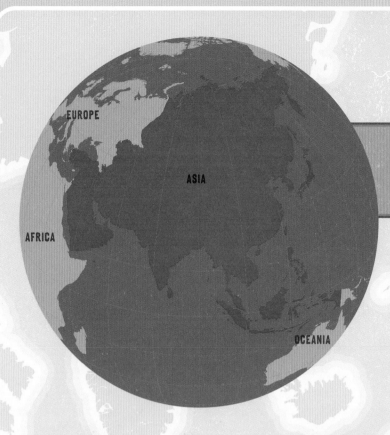

ASIA

Stretching across 44,579,000km² or approximately 30% of all the land on Earth, Asia is the world's biggest continent. It is also the most populous as the continent holds more than 4.2 billlion people in total. Two of its nations – China and India – contain more than one-third of the world's peoples. These peoples are not spread evenly around the continent. Large stretches of northern Asia are barely populated, while there are more than 30 metropolitan areas with populations greater than five million, including megacities such as Mumbai, Tokyo, Karachi, Beijing and Seoul. Nine of the ten tallest buildings and 17 of the world's 20 largest shopping malls are found in this continent, which also features the world's tallest mountain (Mount Everest) and the deepest lake (Lake Baikal).

RUSSIA
Sits in both
Europe and Asia

TURKEY
Sits in both
Europe and Asia

GEORGIA

ARMENIA

UZBEKISTA

AZERBAIJAN

TURKMENISTA

SYRIA

LEBANON

ISRAEL

IRAQ

IRAN

JORDAN

KUWAIT

BAHRAIN

QATAR

SAUDI ARABIA

UAE

OMAN

YEMEN

0	500	1,000 miles

0	500	1,000 kilometres

ARCTIC OCEAN

RUSSIA

BERING SEA

AZAKHSTAN

MONGOLIA

KYRGYZSTAN

NORTH
KOREA

TAJIKISTAN

SOUTH
KOREA

JAPAN

GHANISTAN

CHINA

AKISTAN

NEPAL BHUTAN

PACIFIC OCEAN

MYANMAR
(BURMA)

INDIA

TAIWAN

LAOS

BANGLADESH

THAILAND

VIETNAM

SRI
LANKA

PHILIPPINES

CAMBODIA

MALAYSIA

BRUNEI

SINGAPORE

INDONESIA

INDIAN OCEAN

EAST TIMOR

RUSSIA

Spanning two continents, Russia stretches across the whole of northern Asia and into eastern Europe. It is almost twice as large as the USA. Between 1922 and 1991, Russia was a major part of the Soviet Union, which was a collection of separate republics that have since become independent.

ARCTIC OCEAN

EUROPE
ASIA
AFRICA
OCEANIA

2. ST PETERSBURG

Around 70 cats guard the treasures of the Hermitage – Russia's largest museum. The cats protect the museum's collection of three million documents, paintings and other artworks from rats and mice.

Buorro idit

3. KOLA PENINSULA

The Ter Sami language is the least spoken living language in the world. By 2014, just two elderly people in the far eastern part of the Kola Peninsula spoke it.

BARENTS SEA

KARA SEA

1. KALININGRAD OBLAST

This small part of Russia lies over 400km away from the country's mainland as it is separated by part of Poland. In 2015, large amounts of valuable amber washed up on the shores here after large storms at sea.

4. SUZDAL

A cucumber festival takes place in this town every July. Everything at the festival is cucumber-related – from plays and costumes to food that includes cucumber ice lollies. There's even a speed-eating competition.

MOSCOW 5 4
6

R U S

5. MESCHERA

In 1940, 16th-century coins rained down from the sky over this village. This strange event was thought to have been due to a local tornado picking up a hoard of undiscovered coins that was exposed to the sky due to soil erosion.

7. CASPIAN SEA

The KM, nicknamed the Caspian Sea Monster, was a gigantic half-ship half-plane that flew just 5m above the water. Built in the 1960s, it was almost the length of a football pitch and fully loaded weighed more than three empty Boeing 747 airliners.

Volga river

Ob river

Ural river

9. TUNGUSKA

An area of forest, three times the size of Singapore, was destroyed in 1908. Around 80 million trees were wiped out by a massive blast of energy that many scientists think was a comet or asteroid exploding above Earth's surface.

10. AZASSKAYA CAVE

A yeti-like creature is said to have been seen here in the past and, in 2012, scientists tested hairs found in the cave and found that they weren't human or those of any creature known to man!

6. ALABINO

A sports competition featuring tanks started in 2013. The Tank Biathlon included tank crews from Russia, Belarus, Armenia and Kazakhstan. They had to do laps around a 6,100m-long course whilst hitting targets, and then complete an obstacle course in their T-72B armoured vehicles. Russia were the winners.

8. OZYORSK

For over 40 years during the 20th century, this town didn't appear on any maps or road signs. It was a top-secret place where plutonium was processed for nuclear power stations.

Russia is home to about **142 MILLION PEOPLE** and it's the world's largest country with an area of **17.1 MILLION KM²**. It borders **14 COUNTRIES**, crosses **9 TIME ZONES**, contains **20%** of the world's forests, and just one of its lakes, Lake Baikal, contains **20%** of the world's unfrozen fresh water.

In 1698, Peter I, the ruler of Russia, instituted a tax on beards. Every man who had a beard had to pay a tax of 100 roubles and carry a beard token with him to prove he had paid.

EAST SIBERIAN SEA

BERING SEA

LAPTEV SEA

16. OYMYAKON

Winter temperatures here are often –30 to –40°C during the daytime so the town's solitary school closes for the day only when temperatures fall below –52°C. It must have been a relief when the school got its first indoor toilet in 2008.

Olenëk river

Lena river

15. KHATANGA, TAIMYR PENINSULA

A nine-year-old boy discovered a 20,000-year-old woolly mammoth preserved in a block of ice 300km north of this village in 1997. The 23-tonne ice block was eventually airlifted by helicopter and carried to an ice cave in Khatanga where scientists examined it up close. It's now known as the Jarkov mammoth after the boy's surname.

14. YAKUTIA

The people of this icy cold region enjoy *stroganina* as a delicacy. It is slices of uncooked freshwater fish, often sturgeon or white salmon, that is eaten when still frozen.

SEA OF OKHOTSK

S I A

13. CHARA SANDS

This set of desert-like sand dunes, some as high as 30m, is next to snow-covered mountains and the Kodar glaciers. Visitors can sometimes see the Evenki peoples driving herds of reindeer across the sand.

12. IRKUTSK

Dentist Igor Tsarik makes tiny sculptures of people and faces using the teeth he takes out of his patients' mouths. He has a collection of over 300 of these figurines.

SEA OF JAPAN (EAST SEA)

11. KUZBASS

In 2015, six teams from Siberian cities competed in an underwater ice hockey championship. Players wore diving gear and played upside down, using the underside of a frozen lake's covering of ice as the rink.

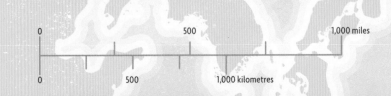

0   500   1,000 miles

0   500   1,000 kilometres

CENTRAL ASIA

China is Asia's largest country. It borders 14 other nations and also controls the territories of Hong Kong and Macau. China is the birthplace of many inventions, including paper and fireworks, and is home to over 1.4 billion people. In contrast, Mongolia contains three million people in a country six times the size of the UK, which has a population of about 64 million.

1. LAKE KHÖVSGÖL

This landlocked country is over 700km away from the nearest sea so Mongolia's navy has just one vessel – a tugboat named *Sukhbaatar III*, that patrols this lake.

M O N G O

Ulaanbaatar is the world's chilliest capital with an average temperature of –0.4°C.

Because the number four is considered unlucky in Asia, many buildings in Hong Kong and parts of China don't have a fourth floor, while 4 is banned from number plates in Taiwan.

2. BADAIN JARAN DESERT

These giant sand dunes, some over 500m high, make a mysterious low, but loud, booming sound when winds move their top layers of sand.

C H I

3. LESHAN

The Buddha of Leshan was carved into the side of a hill in the 1700s. It's so big that each ear measures 7m long and around 100 people could stand on each stone foot.

EUROPE

ASIA

AFRICA

OCEANIA

HIMALAYAS

4. TIBET

Lhasa's Barkhor Street is where Tibetan monks display intricate sculptures that they have created using blocks of butter made from yaks' milk. Some sculptures are as tall as a two-storey house!

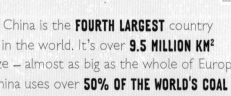

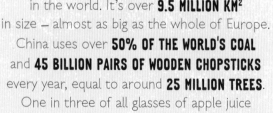

China is the **FOURTH LARGEST** country in the world. It's over **9.5 MILLION KM²** in size – almost as big as the whole of Europe. China uses over **50% OF THE WORLD'S COAL** and **45 BILLION PAIRS OF WOODEN CHOPSTICKS** every year, equal to around **25 MILLION TREES**. One in three of all glasses of apple juice drunk in the world are produced from apples grown in just one Chinese province, Shaanxi.

5. CHONGQING CITY

At the Lehe Ledu Wildlife Zoo, visitors pay to be locked in cages whilst lions and tigers roam free outside! Hunks of meat are sometimes tied to the outside of the cage to encourage the wild beasts to come closer.

Mekong river

6. MEITAN

The Museum of Tea Culture is housed in a 73.8m tall giant teapot. If the pot was filled with tea, it could make over 150,000 cups!

BAY OF BENGAL

16. SUZHOU

Fancy a 3D printed home? In 2014, the WinSun Decoration Design Engineering Company built a large villa and a five-floor apartment using a 3D printer and building waste mixed with cement.

ULAANBAATAR ★ Mongolia's capital city now stays put in one place but in the past, because its people were nomads, the capital moved up to three times a year.

GOBI DESERT

15. THAMES TOWN

This entire town looks like an English town. Completed in 2006, it has Tudor-style wooden buildings, cobblestone streets and a fish and chip shop.

14. SHANGHAI

Artist Red Hong Yi creates portraits using unusual materials. One giant painting of a man was made using 20,000 teabags. It took two months for her to create the 3m x 2.1m picture.

SEA OF JAPAN (EAST SEA)

★ **BEIJING**

13. DONGYANG

Tong Zi Dan is a springtime delicacy made by soaking and boiling eggs all day in containers full of urine from boys under the age of ten. The eggs are sold for twice the price of ordinary hard-boiled eggs.

YELLOW SEA

Yellow river

8. CHANGSHA

Kung-fu enthusiast Wang Xiaoyu cuts customers' hair in his barber shop whilst he's upside down performing a headstand!

12. TIANTAI

Stuck for space, a school in Zhejiang Province built a 200m running track on its roof.

EAST CHINA SEA

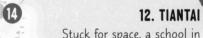

9. FUZHOU

The first beauty pageant for goldfish was held here in 2012. The International Goldfish Championship judged 3,000 goldfish on their breed, shape, colour, size and gracefulness when swimming.

11. DATONG DISTRICT

Modern Toilet is a three-floor restaurant in which diners sit on toilets and eat their food out of crockery shaped like toilet bowls or men's urinals.

TAIPEI ★
TAIWAN

PACIFIC OCEAN

10. TAICHUNG CITY

The Carton Restaurant is made entirely out of corrugated cardboard and so are the tables, chairs, plates and bowls. If something breaks, it's recycled!

Yangtze river

Pearl river

SOUTH CHINA SEA

7. GUANGXI

The Jing people fish by walking on giant wooden stilts. This allows them to get high enough above the water to cast large nets so they are able to reach parts of the water they couldn't if their feet were on the ground.

PHILIPPINE SEA

INDIAN SUBCONTINENT

One hundred million years ago, the land containing India and most of its neighbouring countries was an island. It gradually moved northwards and when it started colliding with Asia, the land buckled and was thrust upwards, creating the world's youngest and highest mountain range, the Himalayas.

This range contains nine of the ten tallest peaks above sea level on Earth.

1. BAMIYAN

Sandstone caves carved in the Bamiyan valley were home to Buddhist monks for centuries. In 2008, paintings dating from the 7th century BCE were found there – the oldest-known oil paintings in the world.

4. KARACHI

At Karachi Zoo a man plays the part of Mumtaz Begum, a creature with the body of a fox and the head of a woman. The man is made up to look like a woman and must stay still in a box for up to 12 hours a day, talking to visitors and telling their fortunes.

The Kashmir musk deer has curved fangs sticking out of its mouth. It was spotted in 2014, in Afghanistan's Nuristan province (2), for the first time in over 60 years.

14. MOUNT EVEREST

In 2005, Moni Mulepati and Pem Dorjee Sherpa became the first people to get married on top of Mount Everest, the world's highest mountain (8,848m tall).

Apa Sherpa has scaled Mount Everest a world record 21 times. And American teenager Jordan Romero is the youngest to climb Everest. He was just 13 years and 10 months when he reached the peak in 2010.

15. ROOPKUND

Over 200 human skeletons were found in the Lake of Roopkund in 1942. Scientists discovered they were from the 9th century CE and had all been killed at the same time by blows to the head from large, rock-hard hailstones.

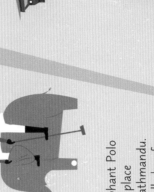

Since 1982, the World Elephant Polo Championships have taken place near Nepal's capital city, Kathmandu. Each of the two teams usually has four elephants and there are two players on each one – one controls the elephant, whilst the other hits the ball with a 2m-long mallet.

THIMPHU

Bhutan's capital city doesn't have a single traffic light ... any more. When a set of traffic lights was introduced in the 1990s, there was so much public outcry that it was removed. Instead, policemen wearing white gloves direct the traffic.

Television was banned in Bhutan until 1999, the same year that the internet was first introduced there.

3. DESHNOKE

Over 20,000 black rats live at the Karni Mata Hindu temple. The rats are sacred, so if one is killed, it must be replaced by a rat made from either gold or silver.

AFGHANISTAN

★ KABUL ①

②

PAKISTAN

★ ISLAMABAD

HIMALAYAS

★ NEW DELHI

③

⑥

⑬

NEPAL

KATHMANDU ★

⑮

⑭

BHUTAN

★ THIMPHU

⑫

BANGLADESH

Ganges river

Indus river

④

⑤

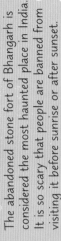

6. PIPLANTRI

People in this village in Rajasthan celebrate the birth of a baby girl by planting 111 trees.

13. RAJASTHAN

The abandoned stone fort of Bhangarh is considered the most haunted place in India. It is so scary that people are banned from visiting it before sunrise or after sunset.

12. CHERRAPUNJEE

Bridges made from the growing tree roots of the *Ficus elastica* tree are used to span high drops above rivers in this area. Some of the bridges still in use were first grown over 500 years ago.

Narmada river

Godavari river

Krishna river

I N D I A

BAY OF BENGAL

ANDAMAN SEA

11. HYDERABAD

The Sudha Cars Museum is not just any car museum – it's full of incredible road-worthy cars in all sorts of interesting shapes, including footballs, aubergines, burgers and handbags. Since the age of 14, Mr K Sudhakar has designed and built over 700 wacky racers.

10. CHILAW

In May 2014, people living in the district of Chilaw were stunned to find small fish raining down on them from the sky.

SRI JAYEWARDENEPURA KOTTE ★ 🔟 **SRI LANKA**

INDIAN OCEAN

Mycena chlorophos can be found in Sri Lanka. It is a species of mushroom with a difference: it glows in the dark! It gives off a luminous green light and is strongest when the temperature is around 27°C.

India is the second most populous nation in the world with **OVER 1.3 BILLION PEOPLE**. An incredible **54,882 POST OFFICES** are needed to handle all the mail throughout the country and India's railways are amongst the world's busiest, with over **7,000 STATIONS, 62,000 CARRIAGES** and **1.5 MILLION TRAIN WORKERS**.

7. MUMBAI

The 1910 Brooke Swan car startled local people. It had the neck of a swan that hissed scalding water and steam, a musical horn that was played using a keyboard in the back seat, and it left behind dollops of whitewash to mimic bird droppings.

8. KERALA

Bull surfing is performed by farmers during the festival of Maramadi. Bulls gallop through rice fields dragging a man behind them who tries to surf on the shallow water and slippery mud.

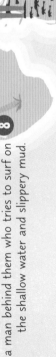

ARABIAN SEA

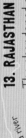

An earthquake in 2013 caused a new island, called Zalzala Koh (Earthquake Mountain), to emerge out of the sea 1km away from the coast of Gwadar (5). The island is about 75–90m long and 15–20m high.

9. MALDIVES

Diners at the 14-seater Ithaa Undersea Restaurant eat their meal underwater inside a building made mostly of see-through plastic.

★ **MALÉ**

🔟 9

M A L D I V E S

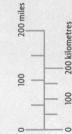

0   100   200 miles

0   100   200 kilometres

EUROPE

ASIA

AFRICA

OCEANIA

SOUTHERN ASIA

This region is bordered by the giant nations of China to the north and India to the west, and was once known as Indochina. It has seen many great civilizations rise and fall, leaving behind hundreds of amazing temples, ruined cities and monuments. The countries here vary in population, from the 6.8 million people living in Laos to the more than 90.5 million people in Vietnam.

2. HANG SON DOONG

The world's largest cave was discovered by a local farmer in 1991. It's at least 6.5km long, 200m wide, and contains its own river and jungle. In places it is over 200m high and the few who have explored it so far have reported clouds forming near its ceiling. Dozens of unknown creature species are expected to be discovered here in the future.

1. XIENG KHOUANG

Thousands of large jars, made out of rock, litter the plains and hillsides of this region. All are believed to have been made 1,500–2,500 years ago. Some measure up to 3m high but no one is certain if they were used to store bodies or food, or who made them and why.

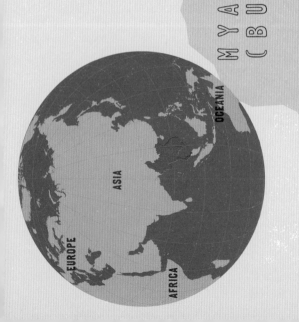

OCEANIA
ASIA
EUROPE
AFRICA

11. MANDALAY

Completed in the 1860s, the Kuthodaw Pagoda contains 729 shrines, each containing one 153cm x 107cm marble tablet inscribed on both sides with Buddhist scriptures. Together, all the stone tablets make up the world's largest book.

M Y A N M A R
(B U R M A)

Salween river
Salween river

NAY PYI TAW ★

10. PAUNGDALE ⑩

General Ne Win, who led Burma from 1962 to 1988, was born here. Win was so superstitious that he walked over bridges backwards and made laws only after consulting astrologers. Believing that multiples of nine were lucky, he introduced 45 and 90 kyat banknotes in 1987 and declared other banknotes to be illegal.

Myanmar is the only country in Asia that, as of 2016, does not use the metric system of measurement. Instead people measure lengths in *let thit* (equivalent to 1.9cm) and *lan* (1.83m), and weight in units, such as the *peittha* (equal to 1.63kg).

T H A I L A N D

In Thailand it is against the law to leave the house without your underwear on. It is also a crime to step on any Thai currency as it is seen as disrespectful to the ruler whose face is on the money.

Mekong river

L A O S

VIENTIANE
★ DOY

V I E T N A M

HANOI ★

SOUTH CHINA SEA

Laos' national sport – *kator* – is like volleyball but played with the feet and legs. A hard ball made of ratten cane (similar to bamboo) is kicked back and forth over a net.

3. DOY

Scientists thought the Laotian rock rat had died out over 11 million years ago ... until one was found alive and well near the village of Doy in 2006.

Every April, much of Thailand becomes the scene of the world's largest water fight. The Songkran is celebrated by people squirting water pistols, even at policemen, and throwing water bombs at each other to wash away sins and sadness, and to mark the start of the Thai New Year.

BANGKOK

4. DA NANG
A 666m-long road bridge in Da Nang is shaped like a dragon whose head spews out flaming bursts of fire. The six-lane road bridge opened in 2013 and, at night, is lit up by 2,500 LED lights.

The Mekong river is home to a large colony of Cantor's giant softshell turtles, each over 1m long. They spend most of their time buried under the sand and only surface to breathe twice a day or to ambush prey.

PHNOM PENH ★

C A M B O D I A

5

Mekong river

5. NUI ONG NATURE RESERVE
A newly discovered frog has large webbed feet and flaps between its arms to help it fly and glide through trees to escape predators. Helen's tree frog (*Rhacophorus helenae*) was discovered in 2009 by Australian scientist, Jodi Rowley, who named it after her mother.

6

A tasty treat in Phnom Penh, is deep-fried tarantula spiders. Other exotic treats on sale here from market stalls and streetside cafes include snake on a stick and egg fried rice cooked with ants.

6. SOUTH OF HO CHI MINH CITY
Built next to a rubbish dump, Suoi Tien Cultural Park is the world's first and only theme park devoted to the religion of Buddhism, and it features dragons, unicorns, phoenixes and tortoises. The staff dress up in golden monkey costumes and cause mischief as well as taking photos of visitors.

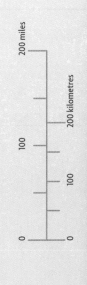

GULF OF THAILAND

7

7. SAIBURI
In early 2010, a pig-tailed macaque monkey called Santisuk joined the Thai police force. Santisuk got his very own uniform with Monkey Police printed on the back, and he helped police at traffic checkpoints.

8

8. SURAT THANI
A monkey training college has been operating here since 1957. Owners pay term fees for their monkeys to be trained to pick coconuts. A monkey that graduates top of its class can pick up to 1,500 coconuts a day.

9. TA PROHM
The temple ruins of Ta Prohm include a small stone carving of what looks like a stegosaurus dinosaur. The temple was built in the 1100s, long before it is thought dinosaur fossils were discovered and understood.

9

ANDAMAN SEA

More than **NINE IN TEN** of all registered road vehicles in Vietnam are motorbikes. There are almost as many motorbikes (**1.4 MILLION**) as people (**1.9 MILLION**) in Cambodia's capital city, Phnom Penh. Yangon, Myanmar's largest city, contains over **5.2 MILLION** people but **ZERO** public motorbikes, as they are banned.

0   100   200 miles

0   100   200 kilometres

SOUTHEASTERN ASIA

Thousands of islands, amazing temples, abundant wildlife, and fascinating histories and cultures greet visitors to these nations. East Timor, Malaysia, Indonesia, the Philippines and Brunei form the region today and range in size and population: Brunei has the smallest (431,000) and Indonesia has the largest (256 million).

14. KABAYAN

The Ibaloi tribe made mummies by placing bodies over a fire and blowing tobacco smoke into the mouth to dry out the inside of the body. Dozens of these mummies, thought to be 500–800 years old, have been found in caves here.

SOUTH CHINA SEA

A type of fruit called the durian is so stinky that it is illegal to bring it into hotel rooms in Brunei. It is also illegal to carry the fruit on buses or trains in Singapore.

10. SPRATLY ISLANDS

Malaysia, Brunei, the Philippines, Vietnam, China and Taiwan all claim they own this collection of over 30,000 tiny islands. And in the past, France, the UK and Japan have tried to claim ownership, too.

⑩

GULF OF THAILAND

ANDAMAN SEA

B R U N E I

9. LAMBIR HILLS NATIONAL PARK

A new species of mushroom that looks like a sponge was discovered here in 2010. It was named *Spongiforma squarepantsii* after the cartoon character SpongeBob SquarePants.

BANDAR SER BEGAWA

⑨ ⑧

KUALA LUMPUR ★

M A L A Y S I A

1. SUMATRA

The largest single flower grows in the rainforests here, but instead of smelling sweet, gives off a powerful stench of rotting flesh! The Titan Arum (also called the Corpse Flower) can grow 3m tall and the smell attracts flies that help pollinate the plant.

★ SINGAPORE

Chewing gum is banned in Singapore.

8. SARAWAK

Deer Cave in the Mulu Mountains contains over three million bats. When they all fly out at night on the search for food, they turn the sky black.

①

The world's loudest ever sound was caused by the eruption of the Krakatoa volcano (2) in 1883. The sound was heard over 5,000km away and the eruption sent so much dust into the atmosphere that unusual red sunsets continued in parts of the world for three years.

3. TUBAN

People in this village eat a dish called *ampo*, which is made out of soil. The soil is pounded into blocks, then baked and smoked in a fire. The local people believe that the soil helps keep you healthy.

JAVA SEA

② ★ JAKARTA

INDIAN OCEAN

Professional hitch-hikers line the edge of Jakarta city to help commuters get to work quicker. Three In One zones are fast roads that can only be used by vehicles carrying three or more people. So drivers pick up and pay extra passengers to fill their car.

③ ④

⑤

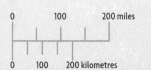

0   100   200 miles

0   100   200 kilometres

13. SAGADA

Elderly people here carve out their own coffins from tree trunks. When they die they are placed in the coffins, which are hung from the face of rocky cliffs. Burials here have been performed in this way for over 2,000 years.

PHILIPPINE SEA

12. MARIKINA CITY

Imelda Marcos, the wife of a former leader of the Philippines, owned over 1,000 pairs of shoes. The Marikina Shoe Museum houses 749 pairs of her shoes and is also home to the world's biggest pair of shoes. They measure 5.29m long and 2.37m wide, and could easily fit 30 regular-sized feet inside.

MANILA ★

P H I L I P P I N E S

SULU SEA

11. CEBU

The Cebu City Zoo offers brave visitors massages performed by giant 6m-long Burmese python snakes slithering around them. The snakes are fed chickens before each massage so that they are full and don't mistake their human client for a snack!

CELEBES SEA

7. TORAJA

Every August, the Toraja people dig up their dead relatives, clean up the corpses and dress them up in clothes to take them on a walk around their village. This ceremony, known as Ma'nene, ends with the dead relative placed back in his or her coffin, which may be repaired before reburial.

6. PAPUA

The Korowai people live in houses made from banyan tree poles that stand as high as 45m above the ground. Until the 1970s, they didn't have any contact with the outside world.

I N D O N E S I A

4. LAMONGAN

Two high-school students invented an air freshener made from cow dung. Dwi Nailul Izzah and Rintya Aprianti Miki won an Indonesian science competition in 2013 with their invention. Surprisingly, it smelt good!

BANDA SEA

DILI ★ E A S T
T I M O R

5. KAWAH IJEN

The Kawah Ijen volcano produces lava that shines blue at night. This is because sulphur spews out with the lava and when the sulphur burns it gives off an eerie electric-blue colour.

This region is packed with islands. The Philippines alone are made up of **7,107 ISLANDS**, whilst Indonesia has more than **17,500**, less than half of which have a name!

Over 10,000 people call the North Cemetery in Manila their home. Rising house prices forced them to move in to their family tombs in the cemetery whilst they are still alive. Some even work from there.

EUROPE

ASIA

AFRICA

OCEANIA

TIMOR SEA

ARAFURA SEA

EASTERN ASIA

There are more than 6,000 islands that form the Japan and the Korean peninsula, both of which have been home to advanced civilizations for thousands of years. Today, Japan and South Korea are economic powerhouses, producing steel, chemicals and vast quantities of electronic goods from smartphones to robots.

In the 1990s, all school teachers in North Korea had to learn to play the accordion. They had to pass a music test before gaining their teaching qualifications!

2. MYOHYANG-SAN

The International Friendship Exhibition is a 150-room museum displaying over 70,000 gifts given to two of the country's previous leaders, Kim Il-sung and Kim Jong-il. The gifts range from an armoured limo from Josef Stalin to a crocodile-skin suitcase from Fidel Castro.

The world's biggest sports stadium is the Rungrado 1st of May Stadium in Pyongyang. It can seat 150,000 spectators. Most years it holds the Arirang Mass Games, which include dances performed by up to 30,000 people at the same time!

The Unification Church often holds weddings with thousands of couples, but at Seoul's Olympic Stadium in 1995, an incredible 35,000 couples were all married at the same time.

NORTH KOREA
PYONGYANG

SEOUL

SOUTH KOREA

YELLOW SEA

3. SUWON

The Mr Toilet House is a two-floor museum and park devoted to toilets. The building is shaped like a toilet bowl and even contains statues of people on the loo!

4. MODO ISLAND

Several times a year between March and June, freakish low tides cause a strip of land to emerge out of the sea. This allows people to walk to Modo Island.

5. BUSAN

The Jangsan Puppy Cafe is full of stray puppies to play with. People often live in tiny apartments here where there isn't room for a dog, so it's perfect for animal lovers who can't have their own pets.

6. SASEBO, NAGASAKI

The Henn-na Hotel is staffed by robots who can recognize visitors' faces to check them into their room, speak words in four languages, carry guests' bags and clean rooms.

EAST CHINA SEA

North Korea has over **5,240KM** of railways, whilst **OVER 40 OF THE 50** busiest train stations in the world are in Japan. **AROUND 3.64 MILLION PEOPLE** use Tokyo's Shinjuku station every day. Meeting a friend can be confusing as there are **OVER 200 DIFFERENT EXITS**.

The world's first portable mp3 music player wasn't the iPod, it was actually the MPMan F10. It was built in Seoul and went on sale in 1998, over three years before the first iPod.

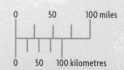

0   50   100 miles

0   50   100 kilometres

Mount Paektu (1) is North Korea's highest point and is a giant active volcano. In around 970CE, a massive eruption blew the top off and sent dust as far as northern Japan. This left behind a crater, which is now a 384m-deep lake.

13. FURANO

Every July, the residents of this town take part in a belly button festival. They paint their stomachs in bright colours to look like faces, cover or wear masks on their heads to make 'hats', and dance.

14. TOKACHI

A fun-loving group here organizes events to try and get world records. One of their achievements was a giant toast mosaic, created in 2013. It was 14.8m tall and 11m wide, and required 16,500 pieces of toast — all made from wheat grown nearby.

SEA OF JAPAN
(EAST SEA)

12. NAGANO

Japanese macaques can withstand below freezing temperatures, but at the Jigokudani Monkey Park they prefer to hop into the natural hot springs and have a heated bath!

The Japanese macaque, or snow monkey, is the most northerly monkey in the world.

8. OSAKA

The Hanshin Expressway travels right through the fifth, sixth and seventh floors of an office block called the Gate Tower Building.

Yoshiro Nakamatsu has invented over 3,300 products — from spring-loaded shoes to waterproof notepads. His Tokyo home includes a gold-plated bathroom as he believes gold blocks out distractions.

J A P A N

★ TOKYO

10. NINOTAIRA

At the Yunessun Spa Resort, bathers can relax in a giant pool filled with red wine! Other pools here are filled with coffee, green tea and noodle soup.

11. MEGURO

The Meguro Parasitological Museum contains over 45,000 specimens of parasites that live in or on other creatures. Pride of place goes to the longest tapeworm found inside a person — measuring 8.8m long!

PACIFIC OCEAN

7. NAGORO

When people died or left Nagoro to live elsewhere, villager Tsukimi Ayano replaced them with life-size dolls made from cloth stuffed with straw. There are now about 350 dolls all over the village, including some sitting in a classroom at the local school.

PACIFIC OCEAN

When taking your driving test in Japan, you can be failed if you don't bend low enough to check for cats lying under your car before driving away.

9. MIYAKE-JIMA ISLAND

The people who live on this island have to carry a gas mask with them at all times because of a nearby active volcano that can sometimes belch out poisonous gases.

13. ALEPPO

Simeon, a fifth-century monk, lived on top of a tall stone pillar for 37 years and was fed by boys climbing up the pillar with bread and goats' milk. Simeon inspired others to live similarly; they were known as stylites, and the Church of Saint Simeon Stylites was built here.

12. HAIFA

Students can study for a BA degree in medical clowning at the University of Haifa. The degree features classes on clowning, nursing, theatre and patient care.

MEDITERRANEAN SEA

S Y R I A

LEBANON

I R A Q

BEIRUT ★

★ DAMASCUS

⑬

Euphrates river

Tigris river

⑭

⑫ ⑪

JERUSALEM ★ ★ AMMAN

ISRAEL

JORDAN

BAGHDAD ★

Unearthed in 1938 near Baghdad, a 13cm-tall clay jar containing a copper cylinder and iron rod may be the world's first electric battery. It is around 2,200 years old, almost 2,000 years older than the first known battery, invented by Alessandro Volta.

KUWAI

KUWAIT CIT

11. KFAR KEDEM

A theme park based on the Bible transports people thousands of years into the past. Some parts of the park are more up to date, though. The donkeys that carry visitors around the park are fitted with Wi-Fi routers so that visitors can use the internet.

⑩

Many of the world's motor vehicle tyres end their life buried in giant holes in Sulaibiya near Kuwait City. This giant landfill site is larger than 55 football pitches in area and already holds over seven million old tyres. It can even be seen from space.

⑨

10. WADI RUM

Rum Farm is not only in the middle of a desert, it also has circular fields. These artificial oases of heavily-watered desert land are used to grow a variety of crops, such as tomatoes, figs, cabbages and squash.

RIYADH ★

9. TAYMA OASIS

Two rocks, called Al Naslaa, balance on smaller ones here. They have perfectly flat sides and are separated by a thin gap down the middle as if they've been cut in two. The gap was probably formed by natural forces, although scientists aren't sure precisely how.

S A U D I

A R A B I A

⑧

Oil is the Middle East's biggest money-spinner, with **FIVE NATIONS** (Saudi Arabia, United Arab Emirates, Kuwait, Qatar and Iran) each producing over **2,000,000 BARRELS OF OIL** a day! One barrel equals about **159 LITRES**.

8. MINA

A giant city of 100,000 air-conditioned tents stretch out through the valley. They can provide temporary accommodation for over two million people as they make the pilgrimage to Mecca, around 8km away.

RED SEA

Y E M E N

SANA'A ★

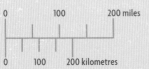

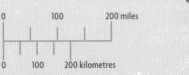

0   100   200 miles

0   100   200 kilometres

7. TEHAMA REGION

Men from the Zaraniq tribe compete against each other to jump over camels. Some can leap over five or six camels. Camel jumping events are popular at weddings and other ceremonies.

⑦

GULF OF ADE

14. KANDOVAN
Cone-shaped rock formations formed from volcanic activity have been turned into cave homes for around 170 families.

TEHRAN ★   I R A N

MIDDLE EAST

Sandy deserts, ancient cities and amazing inventions can all be found in this fascinating region, which is also where three major world religions began: Christianity, Islam and Judaism. The Middle East is home to both the lowest land on Earth — the shores of the Dead Sea in Jordan, which are over 420m below sea level — and the world's tallest building — the Burj Khalifa in the United Arab Emirates (about 828m high).

1. ISFAHAN REGION
In the 16th and 17th centuries, pigeon droppings were used as fertilizer for farmers' melon and cucumber fields. Hundreds of clay pigeon towers were built. Each one was up to 25m in diameter and could hold as many as 14,000 pigeons. Today, about 300 pigeon towers can be found here.

2. SHIRAZ
The Salt Restaurant is well named as all its walls, tables and some of its seats are made out of rock salt.

ERSIAN GULF

★ MANAMA

④

AHRAIN   ★ DOHA   QATAR

③   GULF OF OMAN

3. DUBAI
Dubai has scorching summer temperatures above 40°C but that hasn't stopped the city having an indoor ski centre and a cafe carved entirely out of ice.

★ ABU DHABI

★ MUSCAT

U A E

4. JEBEL DUKHAN
A single 9.75m-high tree attracts 50,000 tourists every year. The Tree of Life stands on its own in the desert, hundreds of kilometres from other naturally-occurring trees. It's thought to be over 400 years old.

ARABIAN SEA

A highlight of the Al Dhafra Festival, in Abu Dhabi, is a camel beauty pageant that attracts more than 15,000 camels from all over the Middle East. Owners of the most beautiful beasts receive luxury cars, large cash prizes and may even sell their camels for over half a million pounds.

O M A N

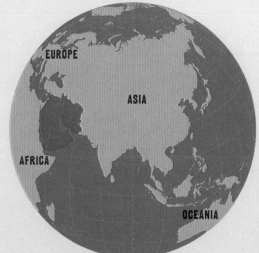

EUROPE

ASIA

AFRICA

INDIAN OCEAN

OCEANIA

6. WADI DAWAN
Haid Al-Jazil is an ancient village perched precariously on a large rock that sticks out of a sloping cliff. Its buildings are mostly made of mud bricks.

5. SOCOTRA ISLAND
This island is part of Yemen and is one of the world's most isolated places. It is home to around 800 rare types of plant. About 300 of these plants can't be found anywhere else on Earth, including dragon's blood trees. These trees have large umbrella-shaped canopies and red sap that can ooze out of their trunks.

This region of Asia was part of the Soviet Union until 1991, when it broke up into separate republics: Kazakhstan, Kyrgyzstan, Tajikistan, Turkmenistan, Uzbekistan, Georgia, Armenia and Azerbaijan. They vary greatly in size but most have rich mineral resources, such as oil, coal and precious metals.

The people of Kazakhstan celebrate three different New Year's Eves using three different calendars: 31 December (according to the Gregorian calendar), 14 January (according to the calendar used when Kazakhstan was part of the Soviet Union), and the 21 March (the Persian New Year).

1. NAFTALAN
A clinic in this town offers patients the chance to take a ten-minute bath in 150l of thick, sticky crude oil to treat arthritis, skin diseases and stress.

6. MO'YNOQ
Dozens of rusty abandoned boats lie in the sand near what was once a busy port city. The port used to be on the banks of the Aral Sea, which was once half the size of England, but has now shrunk to a tenth of its original size – leaving the port 160km away from the sea.

Georgia's capital city, Tbilisi, has a clock tower made from waste materials that looks as if it is about to topple over (a steel beam helps to hold it in place). The tower features a mechanical angel that strikes a bell on the hour.

4. GEOK-TEPE
Kow Ata is a popular lake for a swim – despite being over 50m underground, lying in a cave containing a huge colony of bats, and the water smelling of rotten eggs!

Ural river

ARAL SEA

CASPIAN SEA

BLACK SEA

GEORGIA ★ TBILISI

ARMENIA
★ YEREVAN

AZERBAIJAN

BAKU ★

1

2

3

Since 2011, all children in Armenia are taught chess as a compulsory subject in primary school and there are even chess exams.

2. GOBUSTAN
Gaval Dash is a two-metre-long rock that makes a ringing, tambourine-like sound when hit with a smaller stone. It was played on TV during the 2012 Eurovision Song Contest.

TURKMENISTAN

6

7

4 5

ASHGABAT ★

3. ASTARA
Yanar Bulag is a fire spring. Its flowing water contains methane, which means that it's possible to set light to the water and watch it blaze away. Despite the high methane content, people come from far and wide to collect and drink the water, believing it has healing properties.

5. GYPJAK
The birthplace of Turkmenistan's first president, Saparmurat Niyazo, who ruled from 1990 until 2006, and created many laws. These included banning gold teeth and renaming the months of the year. April, for example, became Gurbansoltan – after his mother.

A shopping centre, a park, a boating river and an indoor beach can all be found inside a huge transparent tent in Astana that stands 150m tall and spreads out over an area of 100,000m² – bigger than seven football stadiums.

★ **ASTANA**

The national drink of Kazakhstan is *kumis* – fermenting horse milk. It is the local custom to tip any milk you don't want from your glass back into the jug so that none is wasted.

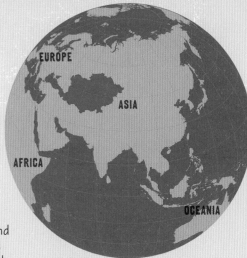

EUROPE

ASIA

AFRICA

OCEANIA

11. KARAGANDA

An avenue of trees stands here, each dug and planted by a Soviet cosmonaut in the hours before they climbed into the spacecraft and he or she was launched into space. The tradition started in 1961 with Yuri Gagarin, the first person to travel into space.

K A Z A K H S T A N ⑪

Irtysh river

7. DARVAZA

A 70m-wide crater has been blazing fiercely for over 40 years. Known as The Door To Hell, it was once a natural gas mine that collapsed and its flames can be seen from many kilometres away.

10. TALAS

The Epic of Manas – a poem about a legendary Kyrgyz hero said to be buried near Talas – comes in a number of versions. The longest contains over 500,000 lines. If this is spoken at a constant rate of 25 lines per minute, the poem would take over 333 hours to read.

★ **BISHKEK**

⑩ K Y R G Y Z S T A N

★ **TASHKENT** ⑨

Syrdarya river

U Z B E K I S T A N

⑧ T A J I K I S T A N

★ **DUSHANBE**

9. FERGHANA MOUNTAIN RANGE

Over 10,000 ancient rock carvings and pictures can be found at Saimaluu-Tash. Some date back as far as 5,000 years ago. No one knows why so many pieces of rock art can be found in this one place.

8. SAMARKAND

In the 15th century, astronomer Ulugh Beg created star charts containing accurate observations of 1,018 stars. This was almost 200 years before the invention of the telescope.

0		100		200 miles

0	100	200 kilometres

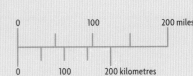

Whilst Uzbekistan is the most populous country (with **29.2 MILLION** people), Kazakhstan is the biggest country (**2,724,900KM²**). Its population is **17.95 MILLION**, which means that an average of **6.5 PEOPLE** live in every square kilometre.

It is against the law in Tajikistan to have public birthday celebrations. In 2015, Amirbek Isoev posted pictures of his 25th birthday bash with friends on Facebook and was fined 4,000 somonis (about £400) by the authorities.

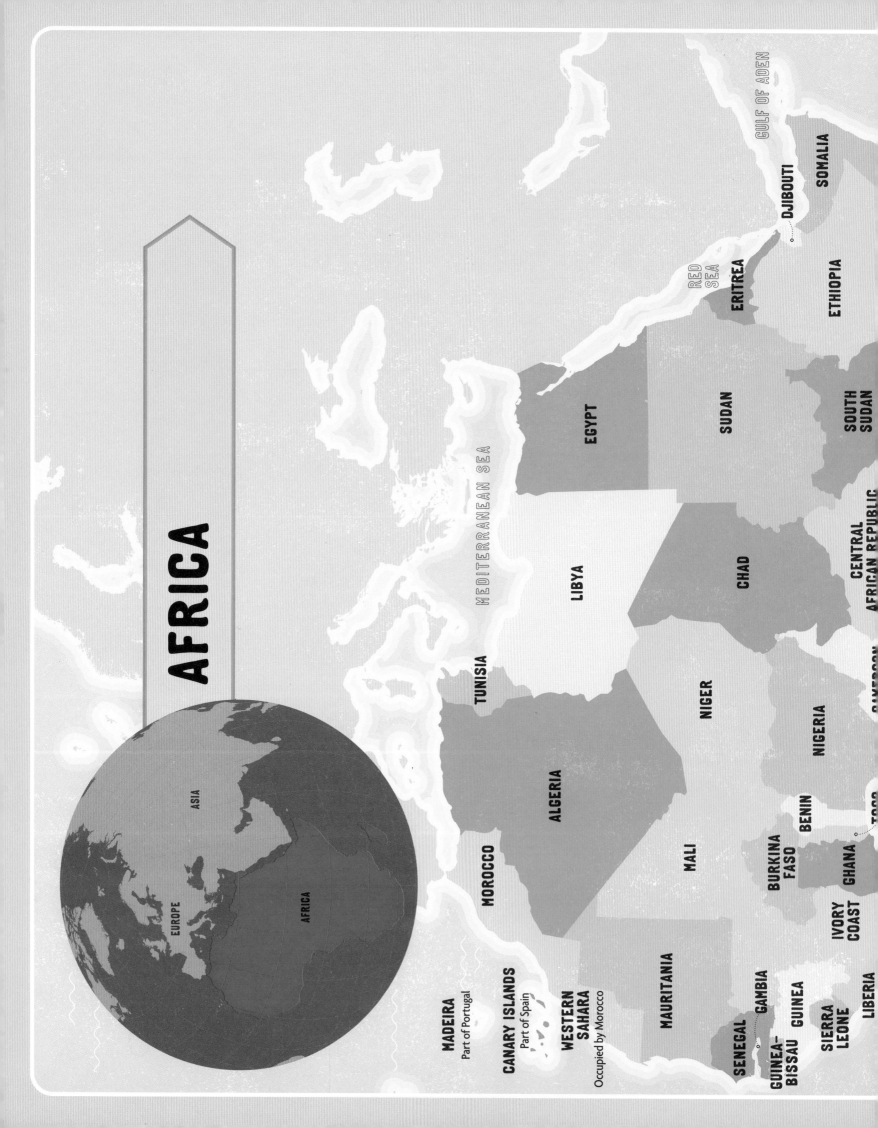

AFRICA

EUROPE

ASIA

AFRICA

MADEIRA
Part of Portugal

CANARY ISLANDS
Part of Spain

WESTERN SAHARA
Occupied by Morocco

MOROCCO

MAURITANIA

SENEGAL

GAMBIA

GUINEA-BISSAU

GUINEA

SIERRA LEONE

LIBERIA

MALI

BURKINA FASO

IVORY COAST

GHANA

BENIN

TOGO

NIGER

NIGERIA

ALGERIA

TUNISIA

MEDITERRANEAN SEA

LIBYA

CHAD

CENTRAL AFRICAN REPUBLIC

EGYPT

SUDAN

SOUTH SUDAN

RED SEA

ERITREA

ETHIOPIA

DJIBOUTI

SOMALIA

GULF OF ADEN

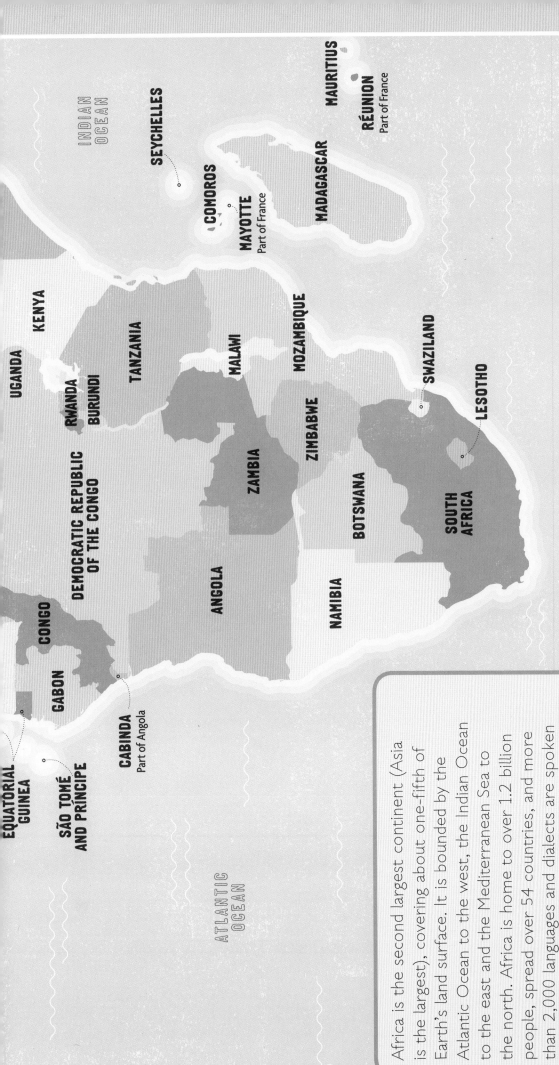

INDIAN OCEAN

ATLANTIC OCEAN

SEYCHELLES

COMOROS

MAYOTTE
Part of France

MADAGASCAR

MAURITIUS

RÉUNION
Part of France

UGANDA

KENYA

RWANDA
BURUNDI

TANZANIA

MALAWI

MOZAMBIQUE

ZIMBABWE

ZAMBIA

SWAZILAND

LESOTHO

BOTSWANA

SOUTH AFRICA

ANGOLA

NAMIBIA

DEMOCRATIC REPUBLIC OF THE CONGO

CONGO

GABON

EQUATORIAL GUINEA

SÃO TOMÉ AND PRÍNCIPE

CABINDA
Part of Angola

Africa is the second largest continent (Asia is the largest), covering about one-fifth of Earth's land surface. It is bounded by the Atlantic Ocean to the west, the Indian Ocean to the east and the Mediterranean Sea to the north. Africa is home to over 1.2 billion people, spread over 54 countries, and more than 2,000 languages and dialects are spoken here. There is a treasure trove of natural riches here, from giant gold and diamond mines to astonishing scenery and eye-catching wildlife, including the world's tallest (giraffe) and heaviest (African elephant) land mammals.

0   250   500 miles

0   250   500 kilometres

1. PARSLEY ISLAND

This tiny island is inhabited only by goats, yet in 2002 it was invaded twice within a week. First, Moroccan soldiers took the island, which is disputed territory with Spain. Then a week later, Spain captured the island in less than an hour.

EUROPE ASIA

AFRICA

★ ALGIERS

MOROCCO

ATLANTIC OCEAN

RABAT ★

ATLAS MOUNTAINS

4. IMILCHIL

Every September, almost 30,000 Berbers come here in order to find romance. If a woman accepts a marriage proposal during the three-day event, she will say, 'You have captured my liver' or 'My liver pines for you'.

2. FEZ

An old tannery in this city still prepares leather the original way. Hides are dunked into large stone vats filled with water and pigeon poo. The high levels of ammonia in the bird droppings help make the hides soft and flexible.

ALGERIA

WESTERN SAHARA
(OCCUPIED BY MOROCCO)

6. BOU CRAA

The world's longest conveyor belt carries phosphate mined in Bou Craa to the coastal port of El Aaiún — a distance of 98km. The belt can carry 2,000 tonnes of material per hour and is the only conveyor belt viewable from space.

MAURITANIA

5. TINDOUF

You'll find goats in the tops of trees here. The goats climb up argan trees in the summer to graze on fruits. The fruit kernals then come out in the goats' poo, which is then used to create precious argan oil used in medicine and cosmetics.

Mauritania is the only mainland African nation whose currency, the ouguiya, is not divided into units of ten. Each ouguiya is made up of five khoums and all of the country's coins are made in Slovakia, in Europe.

3. IFRANE

This town, complete with wooden houses with steep, red, sloping roofs, looks more like Switzerland than North Africa. Nestled in the Atlas Mountains, Ifrane receives snowfall in winter and, in 1935, recorded Africa's coldest temperature — an extremely chilly −24.3°C.

★ NOUAKCHOTT

7. OUADANE

A circular depression in the ground, measuring over 40km in diameter, can be found here. It is formed by the Sahara desert winds eroding rock layers, and from the air it looks like a bulls-eye target. In the past it was used by orbiting astronauts as a landmark when they whizzed round Earth.

SAHARA DESERT BOUNDARY

8. NOUADHIBOU BAY

Many people live in the rusty ships that have been left in the waters beside the city of Nouadhibou. Shipping companies have paid for more than 300 unwanted ships to be left here.

NORTHERN AFRICA

This region contains Africa's largest country — Algeria. Much of the region is dominated by the giant Sahara desert, which is almost three times larger than India. North Africa also features the world's longest river, the Nile, which flows over 6,500km from central Africa through Sudan and Egypt before emptying into the Mediterranean Sea.

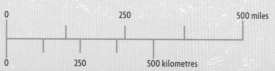

0	250	500 miles
0	250	500 kilometres

9. TOZEUR

The abandoned film sets and buildings that appeared in the Star Wars movies, such as the town of Mos Espa and the Sith Infiltrator landing site, can be found here.

Thousands of mummies were exported from Egypt to Europe for different tasks. Some were turned into fertilizer for farm fields. Around 180,000 cat mummies were shipped to Liverpool in 1890, sold at auction and used as fertilizer.

★TUNIS

T U N I S I A

MEDITERRANEAN SEA

11. DAHAB

Extreme ironing is the sport of ironing clothes in the most extreme environments possible. In 2006, Louise Trewavas ironed clothes at the bottom of the Gulf of Aqaba, at a depth of 137m below sea level.

The North African ostrich is the fastest running bird with a speed of 18m/s.

★ TRIPOLI

L I B Y A

RAMESSES II
Given names

EGYPTIAN CITIZEN
Nationality

1303BCE
Date of birth

KING (deceased)
Job

ramessesII<<<<<<<<<<<<<<<<<<<<<<<<<<<<<<<<
ZE000509,EGY8767875F6725427<<<<<<<<<<08

CAIRO ★

10. WAW AN NAMUS

An oasis in the middle of the desert in southern Libya exists inside an old volcano crater. Three coloured lakes are found along with large numbers of mosquitoes. Waw an Namus means Crater or Oasis of Mosquitoes.

When the 3,200-year-old mummy of pharaoh Ramesses II was flown from Cairo to Paris for fungus to be removed, it had to be issued with its own passport that stated the mummy's job as 'King (deceased)'.

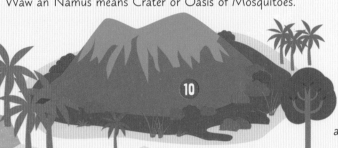

E G Y P T

12. LUXOR

When King Tutankhamun's tomb was discovered and excavated in the 1920s, a huge number of objects were found inside, including a chariot, 116 baskets of food as offerings and over 120 walking sticks.

River Nile

RED SEA

Pieces of pure glass are found in the Great Sand Sea that formed about 28 million years ago. Libyan Desert Glass is mostly the size of pebbles although some come in much larger chunks, weighing up to 26kg.

13. BIR TAWIL

This empty 2,060km² region was the land nobody wanted. Neither Egypt nor Sudan laid claim to it, but in 2014 an American dad, Jeremiah Heaton did. The reason: his seven-year-old daughter Emily had always wanted to be a princess!

14. MEROË

Sudan has over 220 ancient pyramids — more than Egypt — and most are found in one small area to the north. The Meroë pyramids were all constructed as tombs between 2,300 and 2,700 years ago.

★ KHARTOUM

In 2014, thieves stole an entire sandalwood tree from the Sudan National Museum in Khartoum. The tree was valued at more than half a million US dollars.

S U D A N

The Sahara covers an area of about **9.3 MILLION KM²** and contains many sand dunes over **180M HIGH**. It can reach blazing hot temperatures of over **50°C** during the day, but can also dip to temperatures below **-0°C** at night.

The addax is a type of antelope found in the Sahara desert that can go without drinking any water for months at a time. They get most of the moisture they need from plants.

EASTERN AFRICA

This region of Africa is known for its dramatic scenery as it contains a giant split in Earth's crust known as the Great Rift Valley. Inside this valley is a chain of lakes, including the world's longest freshwater lake – Lake Tanganyika. This area of Africa also includes the continent's two tallest peaks – Mount Kilimanjaro and Mount Kenya – and the Horn of Africa, which is home to four countries: Djibouti, Eritrea, Somalia and Ethiopia.

8. LALIBELA

Eleven churches here were each created from a single block of solid red granite rock over 800 years ago. All their steps and decorative features were made using just a hammer and a chisel. Some of these churches are connected to each other by underground tunnels.

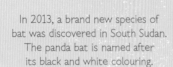

In 2013, a brand new species of bat was discovered in South Sudan. The panda bat is named after its black and white colouring.

SOUTH SUDAN

White Nile river

JUBA ★

Uele river

Newz Beat, a news show on the NTV channel in Uganda features news 'rap-orters' who rap the headlines and summaries of important news stories over a hip-hop soundtrack.

UGANDA

KAMPALA ★

Lake Victoria

Teenage members of the Aka people from the Congo, file their top four front teeth to a sharp point as they believe it makes them more attractive. It is done without anaesthetic.

Congo river

CONGO

RWANDA

① ★ KIGALI

1. VOLCANOES NATIONAL PARK

Mountain gorillas in this park in Rwanda have learned how to dismantle traps that have been set by poachers to capture them.

★ BUJUMBURA

BURUNDI

Lake Tanganyika

BRAZZAVILLE ★ ★ KINSHASA

CABINDA
Part of Angola

DEMOCRATIC REPUBLIC OF THE CONGO

TANZ

At crossroads in Congo's capital city, Kinshasa, human police officers have been replaced by humanoid robot traffic cops. The 2.4m-tall, solar-powered robots have video cameras in their eyes and can send messages and commands to drivers.

ATLANTIC OCEAN

②

2. KATANGA

In the 19th century, 20cm-wide crosses made of copper were used as money. They were known as Katanga crosses after the copper mining region. One cross would buy about six axes or approximately 10kg of flour.

0   100   200 miles

0   100   200 kilometres

Lake Nyasa

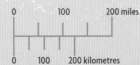
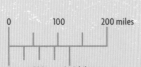

RED
SEA

ERITREA
ASMARA ★

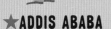

9. AXUM

A 24m-tall granite obelisk residing in the city of Axum for over 1,600 years has been on two inter-continental trips in the last century. One of the trips was to Italy in the 1930s — when the conquering Italian army moved the 160-tonne stone monument. And the other was when Italy returned it to Ethiopia in 2005.

DJIBOUTI
★ DJIBOUTI

GULF OF
ADEN

SOMALIA

Blue Nile river

★ ADDIS ABABA

ETHIOPIA

Jubba river

In 2007, Somalia released a new set of six coins, all shaped like motorbikes. And in 2012 they produced six coins shaped like guitars. This currency is for coin collectors, it isn't for everyday use.

7. GARISSA

Camel trains are used in this region as a mobile library service, ferrying books and magazines to isolated communities and nomadic peoples in northeastern Kenya. The Camel Mobile Library Service lends out around 7,000 books each year.

EUROPE   ASIA

AFRICA

. MAASAI OSTRICH FARM
his farm allows visitors to ride
striches, and jockeys train here
r ostrich races that are sometimes
eld at Ngong Racecourse in Nairobi.

MOGADISHU ★

K E N Y A

MOUNT
KENYA   Tana river   7

★ NAIROBI
6
5
MOUNT
KILIMANJARO

5. LAKE NATRON

A very salty lake in northern Tanzania turns living animals into solid statues. Lake Natron is extremely alkaline and the water can reach temperatures up to 60°C. Creatures who fall into the lake die and are covered in a crust of the mineral natron.

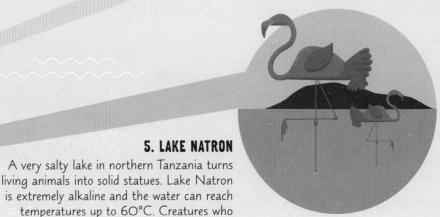

4. MOMBASA

A young Kenyan man, called Anthony Mutua, invented shoes that can convert the energy generated by walking, into electricity to recharge a mobile phone. The Hatua shoes went on sale in Kenya in 2013.

INDIAN OCEAN

DODOMA

3

I A

3. ZANZIBAR TOWN

The Anglo-Zanzibar War is the shortest known war on record. It started at 9am on the 27 August 1896 with a small fleet of British warships shelling the sultan's palace, and ended less than 45 minutes later with the palace surrendering.

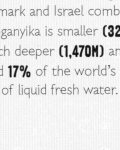

Lake Victoria's surface area of **68,800KM²** makes it larger than Denmark and Israel combined. Lake Tanganyika is smaller **(32,900KM²)** but much deeper **(1,470M)** and holds around **17%** of the world's supply of liquid fresh water.

Francisco Domingo Joaquim, from Angola, is nicknamed the Jaw of Awe for his ultra-wide mouth, declared a world record in 2010. Francisco's mouth measures 17cm and is wide enough to hold an entire drinks can sideways!

When the rainy season starts in rural Zambia, usually in November, millions of termites scurry above ground. Many of them are captured, fried and eaten.

LUANDA ★

A N G O L A

Z A M B I

12. DRAGON'S BREATH CAVE

A mysterious underground lake, over 60m below the ground's surface, can be found in this cave. It's home to one of the world's rarest fish, the golden cave catfish — which is blind and senses the world through touch.

13. LAKE KARIBA

A 128m-tall, 529m-long dam built in the 1950s created the world's largest artificial lake, Lake Kariba. As it filled, more than 6,000 stranded wild animals were rescued, in a mission called Operation Noah.

Giant sand dunes can be found in the Namib desert. Dune 7 is the world's tallest sand dune — it's 383m high.

Cuando river

★ **LUSAKA**

13

HARARE ★

Z I M B A B W E

11. SWAKOPMUND

Imagine skiing on giant sand dunes in the Namibian desert. Well, Henrik May skis on sand dunes regularly and, in 2010, raced to a world record speed of 92.12km/h.

9

12

B O T S W A N A

8. SOWETO

Vilakazi Street is the only known street in the world where two Nobel Peace prize winners, Nelson Mandela and Desmond Tutu, once lived.

★ **WINDHOEK**

9. TSODILO HILLS

In an ancient cave in the Kalahari desert is a 6m-long, 2m-high rock carving of a python snake. It's around 70,000 years old, making it one of the oldest carvings in Africa.

11

Limpopo river

2

10. NAMIB DESERT

The Welwitschia plant grows just two giant leaves throughout its long lifetime. Some plants are believed to be over 1,000 years old.

10

N A M I B I A

GABORONE ★

★ **PRETORIA (TSHWANE)**

8

MAPUTO ★

MBABANE ★

S O U T H   A F R I C A

SWAZILAND

7. KIMBERLEY

The Big Hole is the world's biggest hole dug by hand. It has a perimeter of about 1.6km and is over 215m deep. Over 2,700kg of diamonds have been mined from it.

7

Orange river

BLOEMFONTEIN ★

MASERU ★

LESOTHO

4

6. HERMANUS

This town employs a whale crier, a man who keeps a look out and blows a large horn to alert tourists where to view whales close to the coast.

WHALE CRIER of HERMANUS

5. WORCESTER

The world's fastest grape tramplers attend the Whoosh Festival each year. They compete to see who can crush the most grapes in the quickest time to produce the most juice.

4. MALUTI MOUNTAINS

Despite being a hot country, Lesotho has a ski resort. AfriSki is open for around three months a year and use artificial snow to make the 1km ski run

5

★ **CAPE TOWN**
6

3

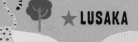

1. MASITALA

This village is full of wind turbines made out of bits of junk. Built by 14-year-old William Kamkwamba — they provide electricity for the people who live there.

Large stretches of Southern Africa are grasslands and plains that provide homes for elephants, giraffes and other wildlife. There are also some forested areas and two large deserts: the Namib along the western coast and the Kalahari in the centre. South Africa is the most populous nation in this region, and it is visited by around 14 million people every year.

COMOROS ISLANDS

Lake Nyasa

Mozambique is the only country in the world whose national flag includes a modern weapon — an AK-47 machine gun.

★ LILONGWE

MALAWI

Zambezi river

MOZAMBIQUE

Over 200,000 species of animals can be found on Madagascar. These include the Darwin's bark spider, whose giant webs are made of silk that is ten times stronger than Kevlar — the material used in bulletproof vests.

0   100   200 miles

0   100   200 kilometres

EUROPE   ASIA

AFRICA

ANTANANARIVO ★

MADAGASCAR

RÉUNION ISLAND   MAURITIUS

2. MODJADJISKLOOF

Visitors to the Sunland Baobab bar can have a drink inside the trunk of a giant baobab tree that is thought to be more than 1,000 years old.

Most football games around the world see two or three goals scored. But at a 2002 Madagascan Premier League game, the result was 149–0! It occurred when one team, SO l'Emyrne, scored own goal after own goal in protest at the refereeing of one of their earlier games.

3. ST CROIX ISLAND

You may think penguins live only in icy lands, but over 20,000 African penguins can be found on St Croix Island near the city of Port Elizabeth.

Researchers at Eduardo Mondlane University in Maputo, Mozambique, are using trained giant rats, with their impressive sense of smell, to sniff out the bacteria that cause the disease of tuberculosis. Each rat can test more samples in an hour than human lab technicians can manage in a week.

Southern Africa is rich in minerals. About **20%** of the world's cobalt, **36%** of the world's gold and **50%** of the world's platinum is mined in this region, and **6 OUT OF 8** of the main diamond-producing nations are also found here. A single mine in Botswana, the Orapa, produces **11 MILLION** carats of diamonds each year.

1. LAKE RETBA

This lake's waters are a dizzyingly bright pink. The curious colour is caused by a type of algae (*Dunaliella salina*) that thrives in Retba's very salty water.

A Chioninia lizard from Cape Verde stowed away in a tourist's suitcase in 2012 on a flight to the UK. The lizard was then thrown into the washing machine with the clothes, but managed to survive the spin cycle, before finally being discovered and rehomed at a UK wildlife centre.

3. BAMBA

Men and boys fish in the lake next to Bamba village once a year only and then just for 15 minutes in a ritual called Antogo. On a signal, hundreds jump into the lake and catch as many fish as possible. The fish are then shared out amongst the villagers.

4. BANDIAGARA

Over 280 villages are chiselled out of the rock face of these 150km-long cliffs. These homes of the Dogon peoples often have extensions to their caves made out of tall, mud-brick buildings with flat roofs, used for sleeping on when nights are particularly hot.

Senegal river

Niger river

CAPE VERDE ISLANDS

ATLANTIC OCEAN

SENEGAL

DAKAR ★ ①
② ★ **BANJUL**

GAMBIA

★ **BISSAU**
GUINEA-BISSAU

GUINEA

CONAKRY ★

FREETOWN ★

SIERRA LEONE

MALI

★ **BAMAKO**

BURKINA FASO
★ **OUAGADOU...**

③

④

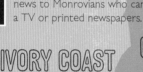

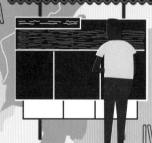

The Daily Talk is a newspaper chalked up on a blackboard that is displayed in Liberia's capital city every day. It was founded in 2000 by Alfred J Sirleaf, as a way of giving the news to Monrovians who cannot afford a TV or printed newspapers.

GHANA

IVORY COAST

★ **YAMOUSSOUKRO**

LIBERIA

MONROVIA ★

⑤

LOMÉ

ACCRA ★

2. FADIOUTH

Thousands of people live on this island – which is made of millions of clamshells. The shells are bound together by the roots of trees.

5. ABIDJAN

One home in Ivory Coast's largest city is a giant concrete crocodile. It was created by the artist Moussa Kalo, and one of his apprentices, Thierry Atta, finished it off inside with bedrooms and living areas.

WESTERN AFRICA

The home of ancient peoples and early empires, including the Songhai Empire, Ghana Empire and Mali Empire, western Africa is bounded by the Sahara desert to the north and the Atlantic Ocean to the west. Parts of its coast were first explored by Portuguese sailors in the 15th century. Western Africa is the biggest producer of cocoa in the world: 70% of the world's cocoa beans come from just four west African countries – the Ivory Coast, Ghana, Nigeria and Cameroon.

GULF OF GUINEA

6. GANVIÉ

This town of 20,000 people has only one building on land: the local school. All the other buildings are perched on stilts in the middle of Lake Nokoué.

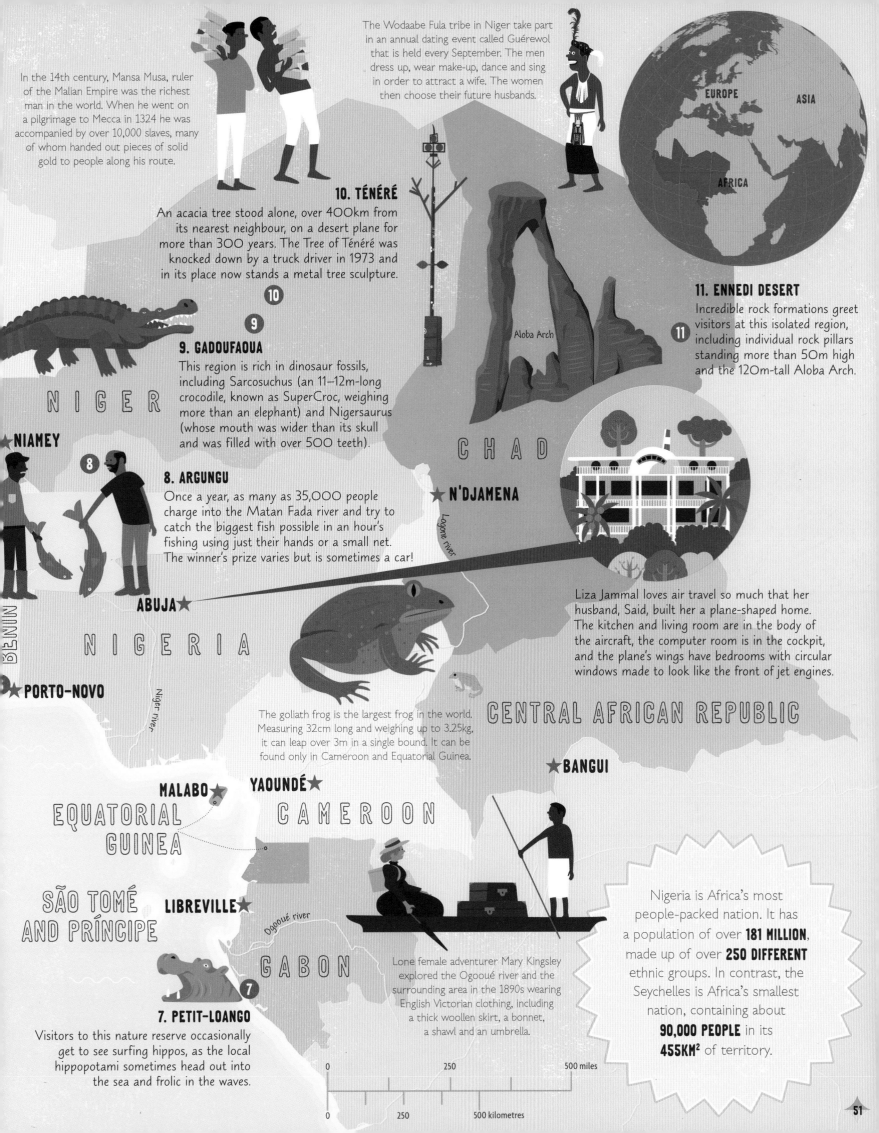

In the 14th century, Mansa Musa, ruler of the Malian Empire was the richest man in the world. When he went on a pilgrimage to Mecca in 1324 he was accompanied by over 10,000 slaves, many of whom handed out pieces of solid gold to people along his route.

The Wodaabe Fula tribe in Niger take part in an annual dating event called Guérewol that is held every September. The men dress up, wear make-up, dance and sing in order to attract a wife. The women then choose their future husbands.

EUROPE
ASIA
AFRICA

10. TÉNÉRÉ

An acacia tree stood alone, over 400km from its nearest neighbour, on a desert plane for more than 300 years. The Tree of Ténéré was knocked down by a truck driver in 1973 and in its place now stands a metal tree sculpture.

10

9

9. GADOUFAOUA

This region is rich in dinosaur fossils, including Sarcosuchus (an 11–12m-long crocodile, known as SuperCroc, weighing more than an elephant) and Nigersaurus (whose mouth was wider than its skull and was filled with over 500 teeth).

Aloba Arch

11. ENNEDI DESERT

Incredible rock formations greet visitors at this isolated region, including individual rock pillars standing more than 50m high and the 120m-tall Aloba Arch.

11

NIGER

★ NIAMEY

CHAD

8

8. ARGUNGU

Once a year, as many as 35,000 people charge into the Matan Fada river and try to catch the biggest fish possible in an hour's fishing using just their hands or a small net. The winner's prize varies but is sometimes a car!

★ N'DJAMENA

Logone river

ABUJA ★

BENIN

NIGERIA

Niger river

Liza Jammal loves air travel so much that her husband, Said, built her a plane-shaped home. The kitchen and living room are in the body of the aircraft, the computer room is in the cockpit, and the plane's wings have bedrooms with circular windows made to look like the front of jet engines.

★ PORTO-NOVO

The goliath frog is the largest frog in the world. Measuring 32cm long and weighing up to 3.25kg, it can leap over 3m in a single bound. It can be found only in Cameroon and Equatorial Guinea.

CENTRAL AFRICAN REPUBLIC

MALABO ★

YAOUNDÉ ★

★ BANGUI

EQUATORIAL GUINEA

CAMEROON

SÃO TOMÉ AND PRÍNCIPE

LIBREVILLE ★

Ogooué river

GABON

7

7. PETIT-LOANGO

Visitors to this nature reserve occasionally get to see surfing hippos, as the local hippopotami sometimes head out into the sea and frolic in the waves.

Lone female adventurer Mary Kingsley explored the Ogooué river and the surrounding area in the 1890s wearing English Victorian clothing, including a thick woollen skirt, a bonnet, a shawl and an umbrella.

Nigeria is Africa's most people-packed nation. It has a population of over **181 MILLION**, made up of over **250 DIFFERENT** ethnic groups. In contrast, the Seychelles is Africa's smallest nation, containing about **90,000 PEOPLE** in its **455KM²** of territory.

0   250   500 miles

0   250   500 kilometres

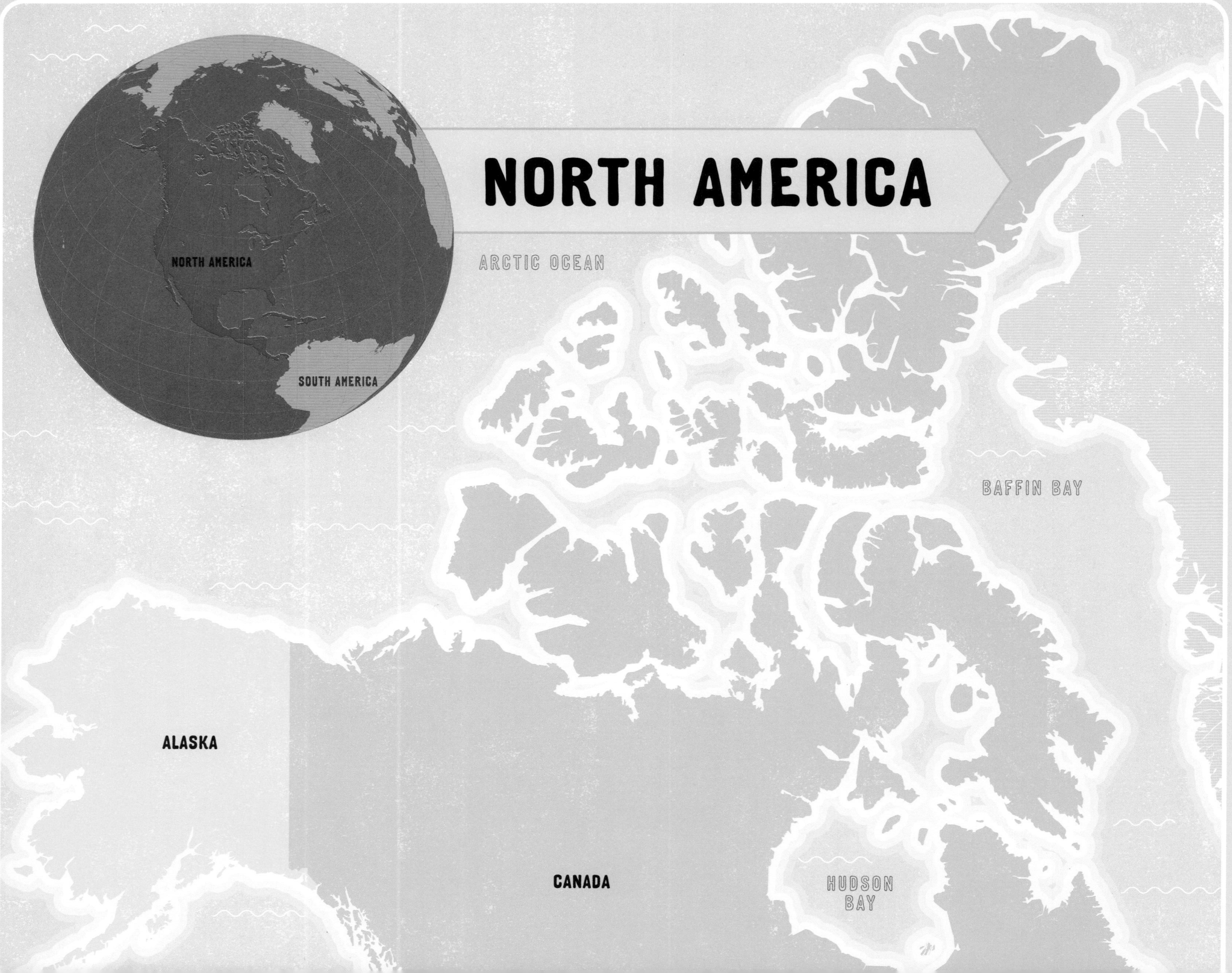

NORTH AMERICA

ARCTIC OCEAN

BAFFIN BAY

HUDSON BAY

CANADA

ALASKA

NORTH AMERICA

SOUTH AMERICA

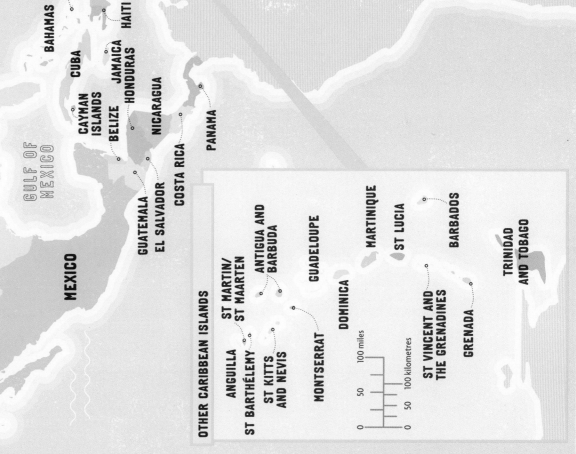

NORTH PACIFIC OCEAN

NORTH ATLANTIC OCEAN

BERMUDA

UNITED STATES

GULF OF MEXICO

MEXICO

BAHAMAS

TURKS AND CAICOS ISLANDS

DOMINICAN REPUBLIC

PUERTO RICO

HAITI

CUBA

JAMAICA

CAYMAN ISLANDS

BELIZE

HONDURAS

NICARAGUA

GUATEMALA

EL SALVADOR

COSTA RICA

PANAMA

OTHER CARIBBEAN ISLANDS

ANGUILLA

ST MARTIN/ ST MAARTEN

ST BARTHÉLEMY

ANTIGUA AND BARBUDA

ST KITTS AND NEVIS

GUADELOUPE

MONTSERRAT

DOMINICA

MARTINIQUE

ST LUCIA

BARBADOS

ST VINCENT AND THE GRENADINES

GRENADA

TRINIDAD AND TOBAGO

0   50   100 miles

0   50   100 kilometres

This continent has it all, from tropical islands and the hot, dry deserts of the southwestern United States and northern Mexico to the icy wastes of Alaska and northern Canada. There are large mountain ranges, forests and plains as well as sprawling megacities and the world's largest freshwater lake (Lake Superior). More than 565 million people live in North America. Its nations also vary greatly in wealth and in size, from the tiny island of St Kitts and Nevis in the Caribbean Sea (with an area of 261km²) to Canada (with an area of more than 9.9 million km²), which is the world's second largest country.

0   500   1,000 miles

0   500   1,000 kilometres

EASTERN UNITED STATES

The Eastern United States lies to the east of the Mississippi river and has a long coast with the Atlantic Ocean. It contains most of the Appalachians mountain system, which runs from the Canadian province of Quebec to Alabama in the southern USA. The nation's capital, Washington DC, is also located here.

Flowing through or along the borders of **10 US STATES**, the Mississippi river starts at Lake Itasca in Minnesota and journeys through the USA for about **3,780KM** to the Gulf of Mexico. The Mississippi contains at least **260 TYPES OF FISH** – 25% of all the different fish found in North America.

In 1943, sliced bread was banned in the United States by the War Foods Administration in order to conserve steel used in bread-slicing machines, and wax paper (used to wrap loaves). However, it was highly unpopular and lasted less than two months.

In Indiana, it is against the law for anyone to catch a fish in state waters using just their hands.

1. CRYSTAL FALLS

The mushroom-based Humungus Fungus Festival celebrates the *Armillaria gallica* fungus found nearby that covers an area of 120,000m² – about the size of 16.8 football pitches and is thought to weigh almost 100 tonnes.

2. HILLSBORO

The Great Serpent is a mound of earth over 400m long in the shape of a snake. It was built around 1,000 years ago.

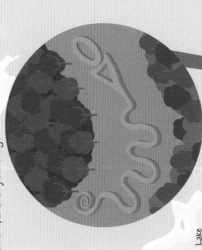

3. PUNXSUTAWNEY

Over 30,000 people gather here every year on the 2 February to see a groundhog called Punxsutawney Phil. If he sees his shadow when emerging from the burrow, it's predicted that the area will have six more weeks of winter. If he doesn't see his shadow then an early spring is predicted.

4. FREEPORT

Surrounded by grassy fields and woods, is a desert-like area in Maine. It covers around 160,000m² and was originally formed by glaciers thousands of years ago. It became a tourist attraction in the 1950s when the owners kept a camel, called Sarah, although she was later sent to a zoo, as she kept spitting at the visitors.

5. BOSTON

The Museum of Bad Art celebrates and displays the worst paintings, drawings and sculptures the museum curators can find. It is near to the Museum of Dirt, which contains bottled samples of dirt, sand and dung from all over the world.

6. NEW YORK CITY

The National Rotten Sneaker Contest has been held since 1974 to find the child with the stinkiest trainers. One of the judges on the panel is a chemist from NASA who has his nose calibrated by NASA once a year.

16. ELKHART

A concrete block full of thousands of human teeth acts as a monument in a street here. It was created by local dentist, Dr Joseph Stamp, who saved every tooth he took out.

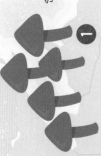

MINNESOTA

WISCONSIN

Mississippi river

IOWA

Missouri river

Lake Superior

Lake Michigan

Lake Huron

MICHIGAN

Lake Ontario

Lake Erie

PENNSYLVANIA

NEW YORK

VERMONT

NEW HAMPSHIRE

MAINE

MASSACHUSETTS

CONNECTICUT

RHODE ISLAND

0   100   200 miles
0   100   200 kilometres

15. SHAWNEE NATIONAL FOREST

Twice a year, during the snake migration, a road through this park is usually closed, so the snakes can cross the road safely as they move from their winter sites to the swamps for summer.

14. BELKNAP

Mermet Springs is a flooded former quarry in which cars, boats, trains and a plane have been deliberately sunk to make an underwater theme park for divers.

13. NASHVILLE

In 2006, Michael Sparks bought a copy of the Declaration of Independence (the historic document that declared the United States a country) in a charity shop for US$2.48. However, it turned out to be one of the original 200 copies made in 1820 and was sold at auction the following year for US$477,650!

12. SCOTTSBORO

Many of the bags and suitcases that are lost at US airports and are never reunited with their owners end up at a massive shop here. Over one million people visit the Unclaimed Baggage Center each year to buy items that range from cameras to full suits of armour and even a guidance system for a jet fighter aircraft.

9. ELBERT COUNTY

The Guidestones are a mysterious monument made of five giant granite slabs inscribed with ten pieces of advice for the world in eight different languages. They were built in 1980 under the orders of an anonymous figure, who is known only by the fake name of Robert C Christian.

★ WASHINGTON DC

The US Presidents have kept all sorts of animals over the years in the White House in Washington DC: John Quincy Adams kept an alligator; Abraham Lincoln kept goats; Calvin Coolidge kept a pygmy hippo; and Theodore Roosevelt kept two bear cubs. Roosevelt's daughter had a garter snake called Emily Spinach.

7. LURAY CAVERNS

The Great Stalacpipe Organ is a giant musical instrument. An organ keyboard is linked to rubber mallets by over 8km of wires, and the mallets strike 37 stalactites to play notes. It was invented by Leland W Sprinkle in 1954, after years of testing thousands of stalactites for their musical tone.

8. SHENANDOAH NATIONAL PARK

Park ranger Roy Sullivan survived being struck seven times by lightning between 1942 and 1977.

10. SPRUCE CREEK

This unusual town contains 1,300 homes, many of which have aircraft instead of cars, and hangars instead of garages. Residents can taxi their aircraft from their homes, down the street and onto the airport runway in the middle of the community, ready for take-off.

11. FLORIDA KEYS

A music festival is held here every year . . . underwater. Musicians dressed as mermaids and mermen play unusual instruments, such as a trombone fish or a shark-shaped harp.

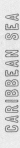

KANSAS
MISSOURI
OKLAHOMA
ARKANSAS
TEXAS
LOUISIANA
ILLINOIS
KENTUCKY
TENNESSEE
MISSISSIPPI
ALABAMA
GEORGIA
OHIO
WEST VIRGINIA
VIRGINIA
NORTH CAROLINA
SOUTH CAROLINA
FLORIDA

Mississippi river
Ohio river
Tennessee river
Alabama river

GULF OF MEXICO
CARIBBEAN SEA
ATLANTIC OCEAN

NORTH AMERICA
SOUTH AMERICA

ROAD CLOSED

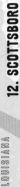

ALASKA

With more than **39 MILLION INHABITANTS,** California is the US's most populous state. Its **76,400 FARMS** produce over 20% of the country's milk, plus over one-third of all the vegetables and two-thirds of all the fruits and nuts grown in the US.

1. FAIRBANKS
Glen and Betty Martin arrived here in 1998 after a 7,644km journey from their home in Dalton, Ohio, on a 1950s tractor that averaged a speed of just 21km/h.

2. TALKEETNA
Every year between 1972 and 2009, this town held The Moose Dropping Festival. It featured poo throwing competitions and it was also possible to buy jewellery made from moose poo.

GULF OF ALASKA

3. WHITTIER
Nearly all of the residents in this town live in a 14-floor apartment block. The building also contains a church, a bar, a police station and a health clinic.

4. SEATTLE
After receiving his ransom demand, a plane hijacker calling himself DB Cooper freed the passengers. Soon after take-off he leapt from the plane with a parachute, but despite a massive manhunt has never been found. It is one of the most mysterious unsolved crimes in US history.

WASHINGTON

6. PORTLAND
In a rock band and have an equipment emergency? A vending machine in this city dispenses drumsticks, guitar picks, amplifier leads and guitar strings.

OREGON

In Idaho it is illegal to go fishing whilst sitting on the back of a camel or giraffe... not that there's any evidence that people here have ever done so!

IDAHO

Snake river

7. BRIDGEVILLE
This was the first town to be put up for auction on eBay. The initial buyer in 2002 fell through, but it was sold on eBay two years later for US$700,000.

BRIDGEVILLE **SOLD**

NEVADA

CALIFORNIA

9. EUREKA
It is illegal here for a man with a moustache to ever kiss a woman. This 19th-century law isn't enforced though!

5. COEUR D'ALENE
The 14th hole of this city's golf course features a floating, movable green that sits in a lake. Golfers lucky enough to hit the green, have to take a shuttle boat across the lake to the green to finish the hole.

WESTERN UNITED STATES

The landscapes here vary greatly, from giant plains and mountainous forests to Death Valley in California which, at 86m below sea level, is the lowest place in the entire United States. The highest point in the US is a mountain peak in Alaska; McKinley (Denali) soars 6,200m above sea level.

10. MOUNT RUSHMORE
The 18m-tall heads of four US presidents were carved into Mount Rushmore between 1927 and 1939. Thomas Jefferson's face was originally carved to the right of George Washington's but after 18 months work, the face was dynamited off the mountain and then Jefferson was recreated to Washington's right!

MONTANA

Missouri river

NORTH DAKOTA

SOUTH DAKOTA

WYOMING

Platte river

Nebraska, a landlocked state, jokingly created the post of Admiral in 1931 even though it has no navy. Since then more than 100,000 Nebraskans have been given the title.

WISCONSIN

MINNESOTA

IOWA

11. GALENA
Les Shockley fitted three aircraft jet engines to a truck. It can roar along at speeds up to 532km/h and uses over 950 litres of fuel per kilometre raced.

Lake Superior

0   100   200 miles

0   100   200 kilometres

0   100   200 miles

0   100   200 kilometres

ILLINOIS

Missouri river

MISSOURI

NEBRASKA

KANSAS

OKLAHOMA

ARKANSAS

MISSISIPI

LOUISIANA

18. TULSA

In 1997, Lottie Williams spotted a fireball in the sky and then, 30 minutes later, was hit on the shoulder. She had become the first American to be struck by a piece of falling spacecraft debris – part of a *Delta II* rocket.

19 **19. PARIS**

A replica of France's Eiffel Tower stands in this town. It was made from steel by a local boilermakers' union and is topped with an enormous cowboy hat.

18

20. AUSTIN

This city installed 31 moonlight towers – 50m-tall towers each with over 38,000 watts of lighting power – to turn night into day. Installed in 1894 and 1895, 17 of these towers still stand here today.

20

21

21. SAN ANTONIO

Barney Smith's Toilet Seat Art Museum contains over 1,000 loo seats all designed and decorated in different ways. Another Texan museum is the Devil's Rope Museum in Mclean – dedicated to barbed wire.

NORTH AMERICA

SOUTH AMERICA

GULF OF MEXICO

UTAH

COLORADO

8. SUNOL

8 Bosco the dog was elected mayor of this town in 1981 and served until 1994. Today you can visit a bronze statue of him.

12. DEATH VALLEY

Hundreds of rocks appear to travel by themselves across the dried lake bed of Racetrack Playa. How they move was a mystery for decades but, in 2014, scientists discovered that the movement may be caused by thin layers of ice forming on the lake bed.

12

17. SANTA FE

A replica of the UK's Stonehenge was created here in 2003 using 200 old refrigerators. FridgeHenge was dismantled four years later.

17

ARIZONA

13. SUPAI

The US Postal Service still uses mules to deliver letters and parcels to residents of Supai and Phantom Town. Both lie inside the Grand Canyon valley where the terrain is too rough for cars or trucks.

13

Colorado river

NEW MEXICO

TEXAS

Rio Grande

16. TUCSON

The Boneyard is an airforce base that is a giant graveyard. It contains over 4,400 military planes – from fast F-14 Tomcat jet fighters to giant B52 bombers – all out in the open in a base the size of 1,470 football pitches.

16

15. SAN DIEGO

A TV channel specially designed for dogs was launched in 2012. DOGTV is designed to keep dogs entertained when their owners are at work.

15

14. SAN PEDRO

In 1982, Larry Walters attached 42 small weather balloons to a garden chair, hopped in and found himself flying high through the air, reaching an altitude of 4,600m and drifting into the flight path of Long Beach Airport.

14

PACIFIC OCEAN

HAWAII

22 **HONOLULU** PACIFIC OCEAN

22. OAHU

Coqui frogs are tiny but have BIG mating calls – as loud as a lawnmower – which can keep local Hawaiian residents awake at night.

0   100   200 miles

0   100   200 kilometres

CANADA

Packed with mountainous landscapes, craggy coastlines, amazing wild animals and historic towns, Canada, with its 9.9 million km² of territory, is the second largest country in the world. Most of its 35.8 million people live in the south, close to the country's long border with the United States.

To protect dairy farmers in Canada, margarine was illegal in the country from 1886 to 1948. Today, it's illegal to paint a wooden ladder in the province of Alberta and taxi drivers in Halifax are banned from wearing T-shirts.

BEAUFORT SEA

| 0 | 250 | 500 miles |

| 0 | 250 | 500 kilometres |

1. DAWSON
A tradition of this mining city is to drink a Sourtoe Cocktail. The grisly drink contains a shot of alcohol and a human toe that has been dried and preserved in salt or alcohol.

2. TAKHINI
At the annual Hair Freezing Contest, contestants dip their heads in hot springs and then let the cold temperatures (as low as –30°C) freeze their hair into amazing shapes. The best one wins.

3. WATSON LAKE
In 1942, Carl K Lindley placed a signpost pointing to his home town in the US. Others have followed to create a signpost forest containing more than 70,000 signs.

Berlin · NEWLON · NICE CREEK · TRACY CITY LIMIT · BLAINE MN · ROBERTA · GABRIOLA ISLAND · EAGLE POINT · FOOL · DANGER · WASACTH BLVD.

Great Bear Lake

Mackenzie river

C · A · N

Great Slave Lake

PACIFIC OCEAN

7. PORT HARDY
Powerful water currents flowing at over 30km/h cause a small island, called Turret Rock (aka Tremble Island), to vibrate. If you tie a rope to the rocks on the island then it's possible to waterski without a boat.

5. ST PAUL
To celebrate Canada's 100 years as a nation in 1967, this town built the world's first UFO landing pad. The cement pad weighs over 120 tonnes and also contains a time capsule that is due to be opened in 2067.

Churchill river

8. NANAIMO
Bathtub racing began here in 1967 and it was promoted by the town's mayor, Frank Ney, who used to walk the streets dressed as a pirate. An international world championship bathtub race is still held here every year.

6. MUNDARE
The world's largest sausage statue is outside a Ukrainian sausage-making factory in Mundare. The almost 13m-tall horseshoe-shaped sausage weighs more than 5,000kg.

Lake Winnipe

MUNDARE

9. MISSION
The wreckage of a single-seater plane has been wedged in the trees of a forest trail since at least 1971. No one knows any details of the crash or precisely when it occurred.

10. MOOSE JAW
A giant moose statue can be found near this town. Mac the Moose is 9.8m high and was once painted bright blue by vandals but is now back to his dark-brown best.

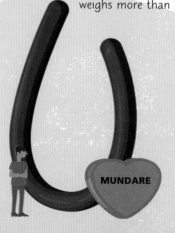

Canada has **OVER 31,000 MEDIUM OR LARGE LAKES** – more than all the other countries of the world combined. Canada also has the longest coastline (**202,080KM**), over **52,000 ISLANDS** and the longest single highway within one country, the **7,821KM-LONG** Trans-Canada Highway.

NORTH AMERICA

SOUTH AMERICA

BAFFIN BAY

4. WOOD BUFFALO NATIONAL PARK

The largest dam made by beavers can be found here and, at 850m long, it's longer than eight football pitches!

LABRADOR SEA

16. STANSTEAD

The border between Canada and the United States runs right through the opera house here. It's shown as a thick black line on the floor of the buildings, which means the stage is in Canada but most of the audience are in the United States.

CANADA

UNITED STATES

C A N A D A

ATLANTIC OCEAN

15. TROIS-RIVIÈRES

Innocent people can spend a night in the cells in what was Canada's longest-running prison (1822–1986). If a stay there doesn't appeal, it is also possible to take a tour round the prison guided by former inmates.

HUDSON BAY

11. NARCISSE

Every spring, tens of thousands of red-sided garter snakes crowd together in packed tunnels and dens in the limestone rock to breed.

⑪

Trans-Canada Highway

13. UXBRIDGE

Pockets Warhol, a capuchin monkey at the Story Book Farm Primate Sanctuary, has proven a dab hand at painting abstract pictures. Pockets' pictures sell for up to £200 each and he even has a Facebook page dedicated to his work.

17. HALIFAX

In the summer of 2014, a robot called hitchBOT travelled across Canada from Halifax to Victoria, British Columbia. hitchBOT's journey included 19 car and truck rides, and took 26 days.

The first person to survive a trip over the Niagara Falls in a barrel was 63-year-old daredevil Annie Edson Taylor, who went over in 1901.

⑰

⑮

⑯

Great Lakes

★ OTTAWA

12. TORONTO

The Biblio-Mat, a vending machine at the Monkey's Paw bookshop in Toronto, dispenses random old and unusual books to customers who put a $2 coin into its slot.

BIBLIO-MAT

⑬
⑫
⑭

14. NIAGARA FALLS

Despite over 2.5 million litres of water thundering over these falls each second, they have attracted daredevils wanting to plunge into the water.

SONORAN DESERT

SONORAN DESERT

CHIHUAHUAN DESERT

PACIFIC OCEAN

GULF OF CALIFORNIA

M E X I C O

Río Grande

Río Grande de Santiago

Balsas river

NORTH AMERICA

SOUTH AMERICA

Found only in Mexico, the volcano rabbit is tiny. It weighs up to 400g and lives on the slopes of volcanoes at over 3,000m high up.

A popular dish, especially in central Mexico, is made from the eggs of ants laid inside agave plants. Called escamoles, the eggs are served inside tacos, in omelettes or by themselves.

15. NAICA, CHIHUAHUA

Crystals are often tiny, but in the awe-inspiring Crystal Cave of Giants, where some are more than half a million years old, they can reach 11m in length, over 1.5m in diameter and weigh more than 50 tonnes.

14. MATEHUALA

In the 2000s, some young Mexicans in this city started a trend of wearing special cowboy boots called trival boots. The pointed toes of some boots are an incredible 1.5m long and curl up towards the knees. Some are even decorated with sequins or small disco balls.

13. MARIETA ISLANDS

Playa del Amor is a secret beach that can only be reached by helicopter or by swimming through a 15m-long tunnel. It was created by a giant bomb blast in the early 20th century, when the Mexican armed forces used the islands for weapons testing.

12. GUADALAJARA

When singer Guadalupe Madrigal got the words of the Mexican national anthem wrong when she sang at a football match in 2004, she broke the law and had to pay a US$40 fine.

11. URUAPAN

In 1943, farmer Dominic Pulido watched the birth of a volcano (Paricutín). A cone rose up out of his cornfield and within a day was about 50m tall! When it stopped erupting in 1952, it measured 424m high.

10. XOCHIMILCO

A small island, called Isla de la Munecas, is decorated with over 1,500 old and damaged toy dolls. They were gathered and fixed to trees and rocks by a local farmer.

MEXICO

About one-fifth the size of the United States, Mexico has a long and rich history as the home of the Aztecs and many other ancient cultures. It now contains more Spanish speakers (about 121 million) than any other country.

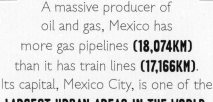

A massive producer of oil and gas, Mexico has more gas pipelines **(18,074KM)** than it has train lines **(17,166KM)**. Its capital, Mexico City, is one of the **LARGEST URBAN AREAS IN THE WORLD**, it contains over **21.2 MILLION PEOPLE**, about one-sixth of the country's entire population.

1. GUANAJUATO
When villagers in 19th century Mexico didn't pay tax on their family members' graves, their dead relatives were often dug up. When this occurred in Guanajuato, perfectly preserved bodies (mummies) were discovered due to the dry soil. They can now be seen in the Mummy Museum here.

2. GULF OF MEXICO
The tallest manmade structure on Earth is mostly underwater. The Ursa tension leg platform is used for drilling oil. Although it stands 1,306m high, most of it is submerged.

GULF OF MEXICO

3. PAPANTLA
The Danza de los Voladores is an ancient ritual that is still performed today. Five men climb a 30m pole. One sits on its top and plays a drum or flute, while the others swing spectacularly around the pole attached to long ropes.

One way that people honour and celebrate their dead relatives on the Day of the Dead is by having picnics in graveyards.

4. TEOTIHUACAN
Once the largest city in the Americas, with over 100,000 people, it was mysteriously abandoned around 1,300 years ago. In 2013, scientists discovered hundreds of gold-coloured balls buried within the ancient city. No one is sure what their purpose was.

5. PUEBLA
Cuexcomate, a 13m-tall structure, was once thought to be the smallest volcano in the world, but it turned out to be one of the world's largest geysers. Now extinct, it has a spiral staircase inside it, for visitors to climb down.

MEXICO CITY

6. CANCÚN
MUSA is a museum with around 500 sculptures, mostly of local people. But the only way to see most of them is by scuba diving, as the majority of the museum is underwater!

7. VILLAHERMOSA
In 2004, this city's council passed a law making it illegal to be nude indoors in your own home. Passers-by who spotted a naked person were encouraged to report them to police. Offenders could be fined about £100 or spend up to 36 hours in jail.

8. OAXACA
Night of the Radishes is an annual festival that grips this city every December. People dress up and many carve intricate sculptures of religious figures and animals out of large radishes.

9. LA ESPERANZA
To bring the rains that help their crops grow, women of the Nahua people have an almighty punch-up! The blood from their wounds is collected in buckets and sprinkled on the land to encourage a good harvest.

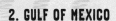

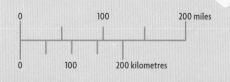

0   100   200 miles

0   100   200 kilometres

1. TIKAL

Three giant temples at this ancient Mayan city have depressions carved into their stone walls that amplify a person's voice so that they can be heard below.

To stop people impersonating police officers in Guatemala, it is illegal for people to bring in police whistles to the country.

BELIZE

★ **BELMOPAN**

2. SAN ANTONIO

Dia De San Luis Rey Festival features people dressed up as deer, dogs and tigers performing an ancient Mayan dance called the Deer Dance.

4. EL SALVADOR-HONDURAS BORDER

El Salvador and Honduras fought a war that lasted just 100 hours in 1969. The war was triggered by ill-tempered scenes at two football matches between the two countries as they attempted to qualify for the 1970 World Cup.

H O N D U R A S

G U A T E M A L A

★ **TEGUCIGALPA**

★ **GUATEMALA CITY**

EL SALVADOR

N I C A

5. SAN ANDRÉS ITZAPA

Water is pumped from rivers and wells, and thousands of kilograms of nuts are shelled every day by people pedalling old bicycles converted into *bicimáquinas* (bike-machines).

SAN SALVADOR

A giant hole appeared in the ground in the middle of the city in 2010 and swallowed up an entire three-storey factory. The sinkhole measured over 20m in diameter and was 30m deep.

PACIFIC OCEAN

MANAGUA ★

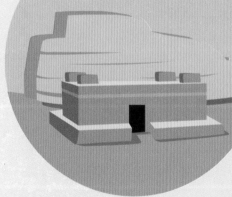

6. JOYA DE CERÉN

A complete ancient Mayan village was buried under 5m of volcanic ash when Laguna Caldera volcano erupted over 1,400 years ago. It lay undiscovered until 1976, but the ash preserved everything in the city, including plants and half-eaten meals.

Costa Rica is the largest country in the world with no army. The country abolished its army in 1949.

CENTRAL AMERICA

This stretch of land joining Mexico with South America is occupied by seven nations and has a population of over 43 million. The stunning scenery includes volcanoes, sandy beaches and rainforests. In the past, this was part of the Mayan and Aztec Empires, as well as those of other civilizations who have left behind ruined cities and temples.

8. CERRO NEGRO

Daredevils climb the 728m to the top of this active volcano and then surf down its slopes using specially-built boards made of plywood. Apart from falls, there is a real ris of the volcano erupting, as it has done so 23 times since 1850.

. LIGHTHOUSE REEF

he Great Blue Hole is a giant hole in the
ea in the middle of Belize's coral reefs. The
OOm-wide hole is 125m deep. It formed
hen the roof of a limestone cave collapsed
housands of years ago.

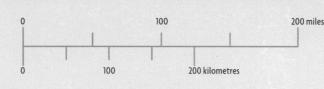

NORTH
AMERICA

SOUTH
AMERICA

Honduran white bats rest at night in leaf tents that
the bats make for themselves. These little bats cut
out the veins from Heliconia plant leaves, causing
them to fold into a tent-like shape that protects
the bats both from rain and predators.

7. COMAYAGUA

People make colourful patterned carpets on
the streets of this town every Easter using
only wood shavings. The sawdust is coloured
with different dyes and formed into amazing
religious scenes, which are then destroyed as
an Easter procession of people stamps all
over them a few hours later.

G U A

CARIBBEAN SEA

9. LAKE NICARAGUA

Bull sharks, normally found in the salt waters of
seas and oceans, have made this giant lake their
home. The lake's fresh water means the sharks wee
20 times more than if the sharks were in salt water.

Central America has
amazing biodiversity. Costa
Rica alone is home to around
500,000 different species of living
things, including more than **850** types of
birds and over **12,000** species of plants.
Despite only covering **0.03%** of the
Earth's surface, Costa Rica
contains over **4%** of all the
world's living things.

12. PANAMA CANAL

In 1928, the lowest toll or fee to travel down
the Panama Canal was paid by American
adventurer, Richard Halliburton. He paid
just 36 US cents as he had no boat and
was swimming the entire length of the canal!
His swim took 50 hours to complete.

10. MOUNT IZARÚ

The peak of this 3,432m-high mountain is
one of the few places in the world that you
can stand and view both the Pacific Ocean
and the Atlantic Ocean.

SAN JOSE ★

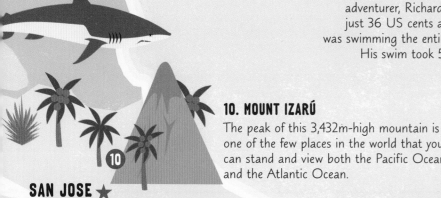

COSTA RICA

Panama Canal ⑫

★ **PANAMA CITY**

In 2015, potholes on the city streets sent tweets
(Twitter messages) to the city council every time
a car tyre rolled over them. Motion-sensing devices
were installed in many potholes by a TV news show,
Telemetro Reporta, to highlight the many holes that
had developed in the roads.

Every radio station in
Costa Rica plays the country's
national anthem every morning
at 7 o'clock precisely.

P A N A M A ⑪

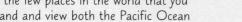

The Panamanian golden frog often
lives near loud waterfalls where the
noise of crashing water drowns
out its call. So, to communicate
with other frogs, it waves!

11. OLA

The Valley of Square Trees lives up to its
name, as it contains dozens of cottonwood
trees that have grown with square trunks,
many with perfect right-angled corners.

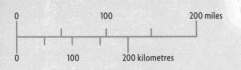

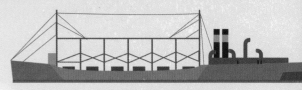

1. BIG MAJOR CAY

Pigs don't normally venture into water but the wild pigs on this small, uninhabited island do. They regularly swim out to sea, just to lark about in the water or to collect food dumped overboard by boats and ships.

★ NASSAU

2. BERMUDA TRIANGLE

Part of the Caribbean, the Bermuda Triangle is infamous because many planes and ships seem to have disappeared there. These include the USS *Cyclops* and its 300 or so crew in 1918 and a squadron of US Navy bomber aircraft in 1945.

★ HAVANA

B A H A M A S

When coming to power in Cuba in 1959, one of Fidel Castro's first acts was to ban the board game Monopoly and have every set on Cuba destroyed. Christmas was also not celebrated as a holiday in Cuba until 1997.

C U B A

T U R K S   A N D
C A I C O S
I S L A N D S

C A Y M A N
I S L A N D S

THE ISLAND OF
HISPANIOLA (DIVIDED
INTO HAITI AND THE
DOMINICAN REPUBLIC)

H A I T I

PORT-AU-PRINCE ★

JAMAICA ★ KINGSTON

CARIBBEAN

Over 7,000 islands, big and small, are dotted through the Caribbean Sea to the east of Central America. Most enjoy a warm, tropical climate and some of these islands were the first land in the Americas to be discovered by explorers from Europe.

3. PORT ROYAL

In the 17th century, Port Royal was a popular haunt of pirates and smugglers. In 1692, a giant earthquake caused the ground to swallow up over two-thirds of the city with the remainder battered by a giant tsunami. In the 1960s, a pocket watch was found on the seafloor that had stopped at 11.43am – the time of the earthquake.

Tourism is a major industry in the Caribbean. A record **5,141,377** people visited the Dominican Republic in 2014, the highest number for any Caribbean nation, followed by **3,001,958** to Cuba and **2,080,181** to Jamaica. Even tiny Aruba, just **179KM²** in size – about the area of Washington DC – received **1,072,082** tourists in 2014.

NORTH
AMERICA

SOUTH
AMERICA

The Hispaniolan solenodon, found only on Hispaniola (the island shared by Haiti and the Dominican Republic), has a long snout that is joined to its skull by a ball-and-socket joint. This allows it to point its snout in all directions. It also has toxic saliva!

4. ARECIBO

A 305m-wide dish built into the mountainside has been the world's largest single-dish radio telescope for over 50 years. Made up of almost 40,000 aluminium panels, the Arecibo Radio Telescope helped beam 1,679 pieces of information to outer space in 1974, which included a stick figure of a human and Earth's place in the solar system.

5. GINGER ISLAND

Odd coral, shaped like giant mushrooms and tall organ pipes, can be found at the Alice in Wonderland dive site, just off the coast of Ginger Island, part of the British Virgin Islands.

6. ST MARTIN

Holidaymakers on Maho Beach get up close and personal with giant airliners many times each day, as the runway of Princess Juliana International Airport starts just a few paces away from the beach. Giant jumbo jets fly just metres overhead.

7. DELICES

A mountain lake normally offers cold, refreshing water, but the lake on top of Watt Mountain is different. It is connected below to an opening in the Earth's crust where heat keeps the water in the centre of Boiling Lake at boiling point.

8. MARTINIQUE

When the Mount Pelée volcano erupted violently in 1902, all 30,000 inhabitants of the town of St Pierre at the base of the volcano perished with the exception of one – Ludger Sylbaris. He was being held overnight as the sole prisoner in the town's jail.

9. GRENADA

To see Jason deCaires Taylor's sculpture exhibition, you'll need a mask and snorkel or diving suit. Over 60 sculptures, mostly of people, form the Underwater Sculpture Park. They are anchored to the seafloor in Molinère Bay.

10. LA BREA

A giant lake of liquid asphalt (the material used to cover road surfaces) can be found here bubbling and hissing away. Pitch Lake is almost 100m deep and is thought to contain as much as nine million tonnes of asphalt. Visitors can walk on the parts of its surface that have hardened into a crust.

Members of the Dominican Republic's armed forces are not allowed to vote in elections for government. Neither are the police.

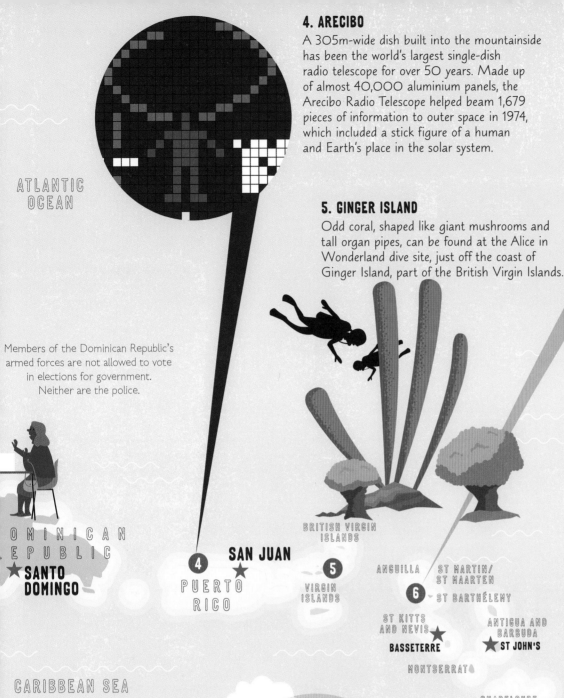

ATLANTIC OCEAN

DOMINICAN REPUBLIC

★ SANTO DOMINGO

CARIBBEAN SEA

SAN JUAN ★

4

PUERTO RICO

5

VIRGIN ISLANDS

BRITISH VIRGIN ISLANDS

ANGUILLA

ST MARTIN/ ST MAARTEN

6

ST BARTHÉLEMY

ST KITTS AND NEVIS ★
BASSETERRE

ANTIGUA AND BARBUDA
★ ST JOHN'S

MONTSERRAT

GUADELOUPE

DOMINICA

ROSEAU ★ 7

MARTINIQUE 8
FORT-DE-FRANCE ★

ST LUCIA ★ CASTRIES

ST VINCENT AND THE GRENADINES

BARBADOS

KINGSTOWN ★

BRIDGETOWN ★

ARUBA

CURAÇAO

9 GRENADA
★ ST GEORGE'S

TRINIDAD AND TOBAGO

PORT OF SPAIN ★

10

SOUTH AMERICA

NORTH ATLANTIC OCEAN

FRENCH GUIANA

SURINAME

GUYANA

VENEZUELA

BRAZIL

COLOMBIA

PERU

ECUADOR

NORTH AMERICA

SOUTH AMERICA

ANTARCTICA

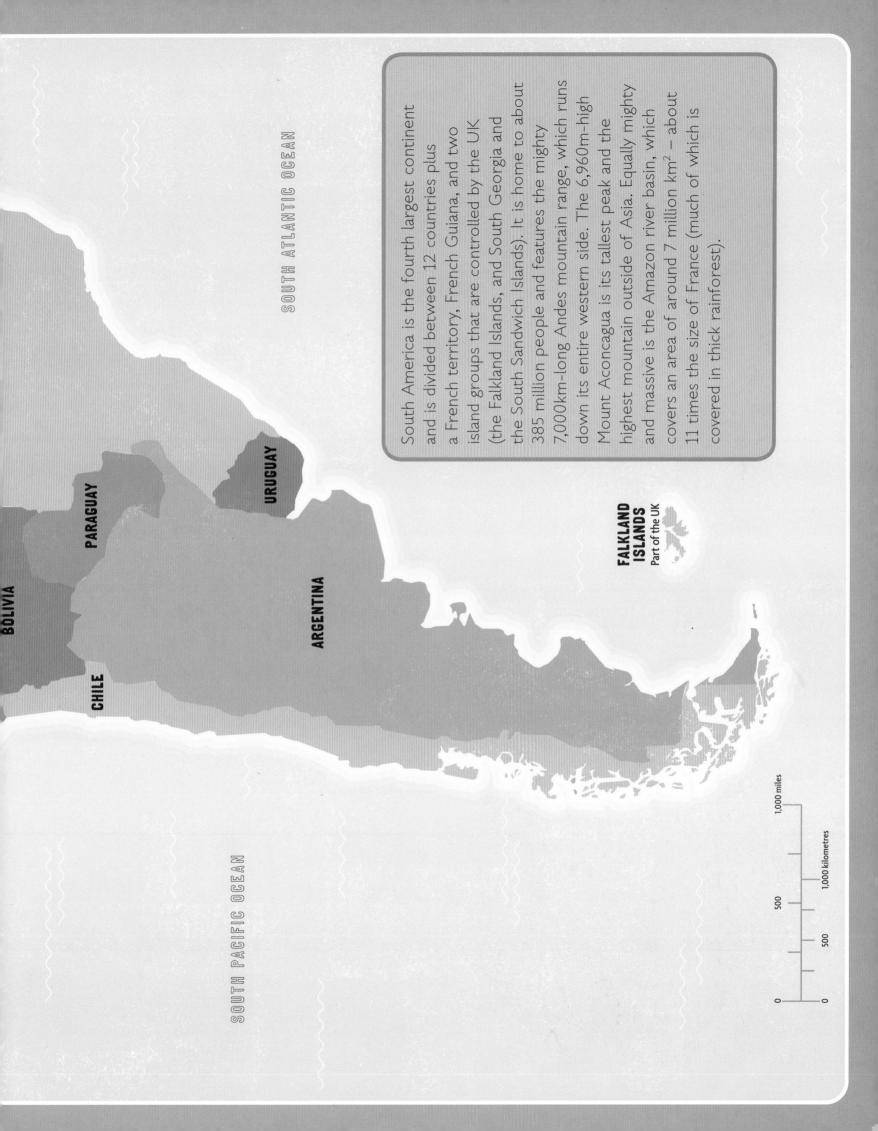

SOUTH ATLANTIC OCEAN

SOUTH PACIFIC OCEAN

BOLIVIA

PARAGUAY

URUGUAY

CHILE

ARGENTINA

FALKLAND ISLANDS
Part of the UK

South America is the fourth largest continent and is divided between 12 countries plus a French territory, French Guiana, and two island groups that are controlled by the UK (the Falkland Islands, and South Georgia and the South Sandwich Islands). It is home to about 385 million people and features the mighty 7,000km-long Andes mountain range, which runs down its entire western side. The 6,960m-high Mount Aconcagua is its tallest peak and the highest mountain outside of Asia. Equally mighty and massive is the Amazon river basin, which covers an area of around 7 million km² – about 11 times the size of France (much of which is covered in thick rainforest).

0   500   1,000 miles

0   500   1,000 kilometres

1. LAKE MARACAIBO

Thunder and lightning storms rage for up to 300 nights a year, every year, over a small region of Venezuela. They occur where the Catatumbo river empties into Lake Maracaibo. Each year an estimated 1.2 million lightning strikes occur, which can be seen from over 400km away.

A speciality of Colombia is *aguapanela con queso* – a hot drink made from sugar cane into which people dunk a piece of stinky, fermented cheese.

2. MEDELLÍN

In 2011, chef Juan Manuel Barrientos made and displayed two beautiful wedding dresses fashioned from sugar-glazed rose petals that could be eaten.

★ BOGOTÁ

3. ICONONZO

The mayor of this Colombian town made gossiping against the law in 2005. Those found guilty of persistent gossiping can face fines of as much as £50,000 and up to four years in prison.

4. CANO CRISTALES

Between September and November each year, the Cano Cristales river becomes a riot of colour. The *macarenia clavigera* algae, together with other plants in the riverbed, turn it into a rainbow of colours.

5. IPIALES

Las Lajas Sanctuary is a giant cathedral built in a deep canyon where the Guáitara river flows. It is connected to a 50m-tall bridge on the other side. The cathedral appears to hover in the middle of the canyon.

★ CARACAS

In 2011, about 120 mime artists dressed as clowns were let loose on the streets of Caracas to help control the road traffic. The artists waved their fingers at dangerous drivers and pedestrians who didn't cross the road carefully.

6. MÉRIDA

Heladeria Coromoto sells more than 850 flavours of ice cream, from vanilla and mango to macaroni cheese, garlic and sardines in brandy!

Discovered in 2009 by a scientist from Kyrgyzstan, the Venezuelan poodle moth is covered in thick, whitish fur, making it loo more like a mammal with wings than a moth At first, some scientists thought it was a hoa

CARIBBEAN SEA

V E N E

C O L O M B I A

Magdalena river

Meta river

Guainía river

Caquetá river

Amazon river

NORTH AMERICA

SOUTH AMERICA

ANTARCTICA

7. KOUROU

A beach on the French Guiana coast is covered in green-coloured sand. This unusual sand is believed to be caused by a mineral, called olivine, which is formed by volcanic lava when it cools in seawater.

ATLANTIC OCEAN

Orinoco river

A mysterious insect was discovered in the jungles of Suriname in 2013 with a tail like a shaving brush. The 5mm-long creature has mystified scientists who think that the creature is in its nymph stage as the adult insect would have wings.

Z U E L A

GEORGETOWN ★

Homestretch Avenue in Georgetown is closed every Sunday so that draymen can hold donkey or mule races.

★ PARAMARIBO

G U Y A N A   S U R I N A M E

The hoatzin is Guyana's national bird. It is one of the few birds that eats leaves as its main food and digests food like a cow. A meal takes 45 hours to pass through the bird, which makes them smell of manure – giving them their nickname stinkbirds.

CAYENNE ★

Kings Carnival includes parades that feature some odd characters, including zombies, people dressed up as bat-like creatures called *Soussouris*, and men covered in sticky molasses or grease, who try to grab and hug spectators.

Orinoco river

The Surinam horned frog is about 10–20cm long and has a mouth 1.6 times wider than the length of its body. Babies hatch in pockets in the female toad's skin, causing the skin to wriggle and ripple around before the babies grow and leave their mother.

F R E N C H
G U I A N A

NORTHERN SOUTH AMERICA

Northern South America (Venezuela, Guyana, Suriname, French Guiana and Colombia) is home to scenic cloud forests, bustling cities — such as Caracas and Bogotá — and the world's tallest waterfall, Angel Falls in Venezuela, which has a spectacular 979m drop. Much of the region is sparsely populated. Guyana, for example, is more than 80,000km² larger than England, but its population of around 735,500 is less than 1/70th of England's.

For a country of just over half a million people, Suriname has a lot of official languages, including Dutch, Javanese and Hindustani.

Two dishes eaten in French Guiana are braised cow heel and iguana soup, which contains large chunks of iguana lizards.

With an area of **163,821KM²** and a population of about **558,000**, Suriname is South America's smallest and least populous independent nation. In contrast, there are about **8 MILLION** people in Colombia's capital city, Bogotá.

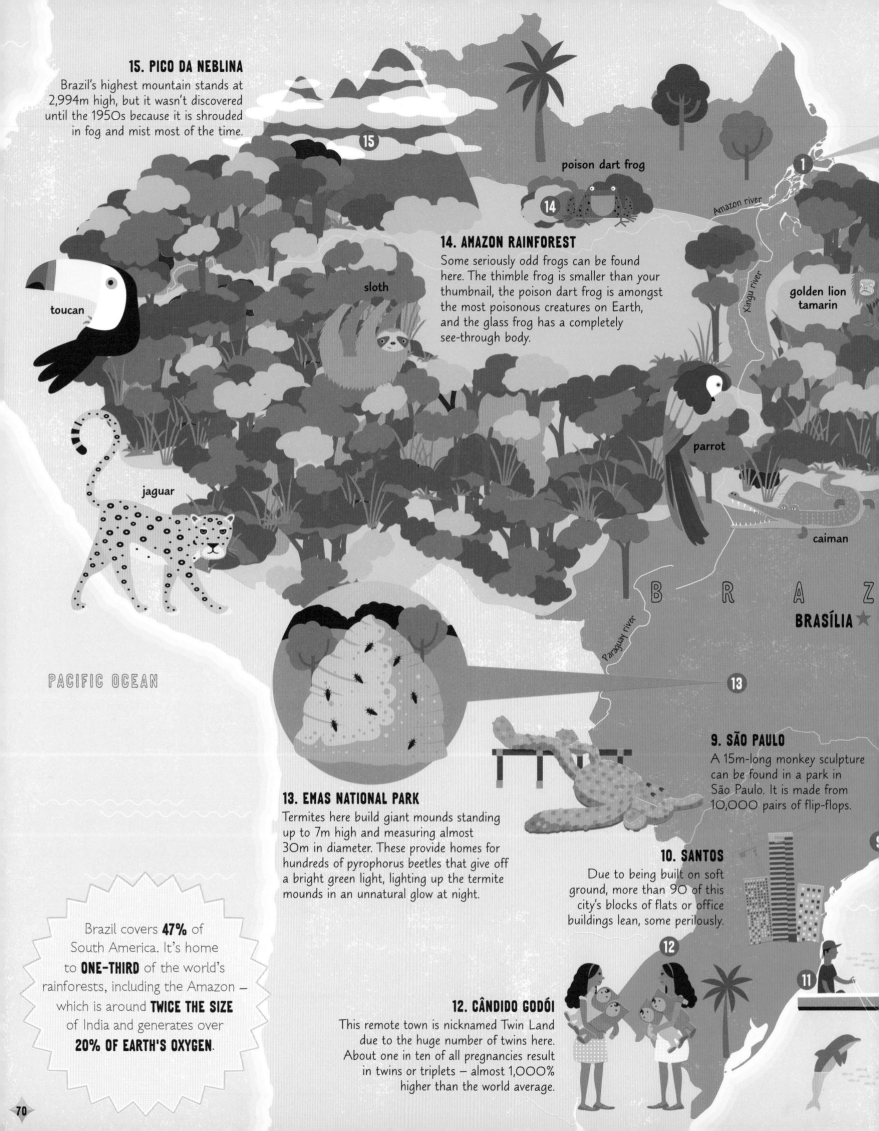

15. PICO DA NEBLINA
Brazil's highest mountain stands at 2,994m high, but it wasn't discovered until the 1950s because it is shrouded in fog and mist most of the time.

15

toucan

sloth

jaguar

PACIFIC OCEAN

poison dart frog

14

14. AMAZON RAINFOREST
Some seriously odd frogs can be found here. The thimble frog is smaller than your thumbnail, the poison dart frog is amongst the most poisonous creatures on Earth, and the glass frog has a completely see-through body.

Amazon river

Xingu river

golden lion tamarin

parrot

caiman

B R A Z

BRASÍLIA ★

Paraguay river

13

13. EMAS NATIONAL PARK
Termites here build giant mounds standing up to 7m high and measuring almost 30m in diameter. These provide homes for hundreds of pyrophorus beetles that give off a bright green light, lighting up the termite mounds in an unnatural glow at night.

9. SÃO PAULO
A 15m-long monkey sculpture can be found in a park in São Paulo. It is made from 10,000 pairs of flip-flops.

10. SANTOS
Due to being built on soft ground, more than 90 of this city's blocks of flats or office buildings lean, some perilously.

12

11

Brazil covers **47%** of South America. It's home to **ONE-THIRD** of the world's rainforests, including the Amazon — which is around **TWICE THE SIZE** of India and generates over **20% OF EARTH'S OXYGEN**.

12. CÂNDIDO GODÓI
This remote town is nicknamed Twin Land due to the huge number of twins here. About one in ten of all pregnancies result in twins or triplets — almost 1,000% higher than the world average.

1. AMAZON RIVER

The Amazon river flows into the Atlantic Ocean, but twice a year tides from the ocean flow up the river. These tides create an almost never-ending wave, known as the pororoca, on which daredevils try to surf. The wave can travel hundreds of kilometres at speeds of 30km/h.

Named by Portuguese explorers after the Brazilwood tree found on the coast, Brazil is the giant of South America and the fifth largest country in the world. More than 204 million people live here — in environments that range from coastal plains and big, sprawling cities to rugged mountains and lush rainforest crossed by thousands of rivers.

2. SOBRAL

In 2011, Sobral prison started using geese as security guards. The geese make a lot of noise when they detect unexpected movements, such as prisoners fighting or trying to escape.

3. INGÁ

The Ingá Stone is a mysterious 46m-long, 3.8m-high stone slab covered with carvings thought to be 6,000 years old. Some people claim that the carvings show star systems a long way from Earth and even flying machines.

4. PARAIBA

Two parents in Paraiba named all 15 of their children after the father, Walter. All nine daughters and six sons were given his name: including Walterlucia, Walterlivia, Walterlenia, Walterlonia, Walterluis and Walteroliv.

5. RECIFE

To stop trouble amongst fans, football club Sport Club do Recife hired and trained the fans' own mothers as security guards for a match in 2015. They wore orange vests with 'Security Mum' in Portuguese printed on them. There was no trouble at the game as a result.

ATLANTIC OCEAN

6. PEDRA AZUL

An expensive ground coffee went on sale here in 2012 for almost £300 per kilogram. It was made from coffee beans that had been chewed and then spat out by gray four-eyed opossums.

7. NOIVA DO CORDEIRO

There are about 600 women in this farming town, but hardly any men. It was founded by a woman in 1891, and all land and crops are shared. Any husbands of the women work away from the community and are only allowed to visit at weekends.

Paraná river

TOTALLY LOST!

8. RIO DE JANEIRO

An elephant seal normally found in the waters around Antarctica got seriously lost in 2013 and ended up in Rio de Janeiro. It even crossed a pedestrian crossing on its 90-minute tour of the city, before it headed back to the ocean.

NORTH AMERICA

SOUTH AMERICA

ANTARCTICA

11. LAGUNA

Around 20 wild bottlenose dolphins work with fishermen so that both can have a fish supper. The dolphins herd shoals of mullet towards the fishermen and even bob their heads and fins when they think they should throw the nets.

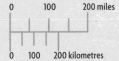

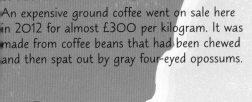

0	100	200 miles

0	100	200 kilometres

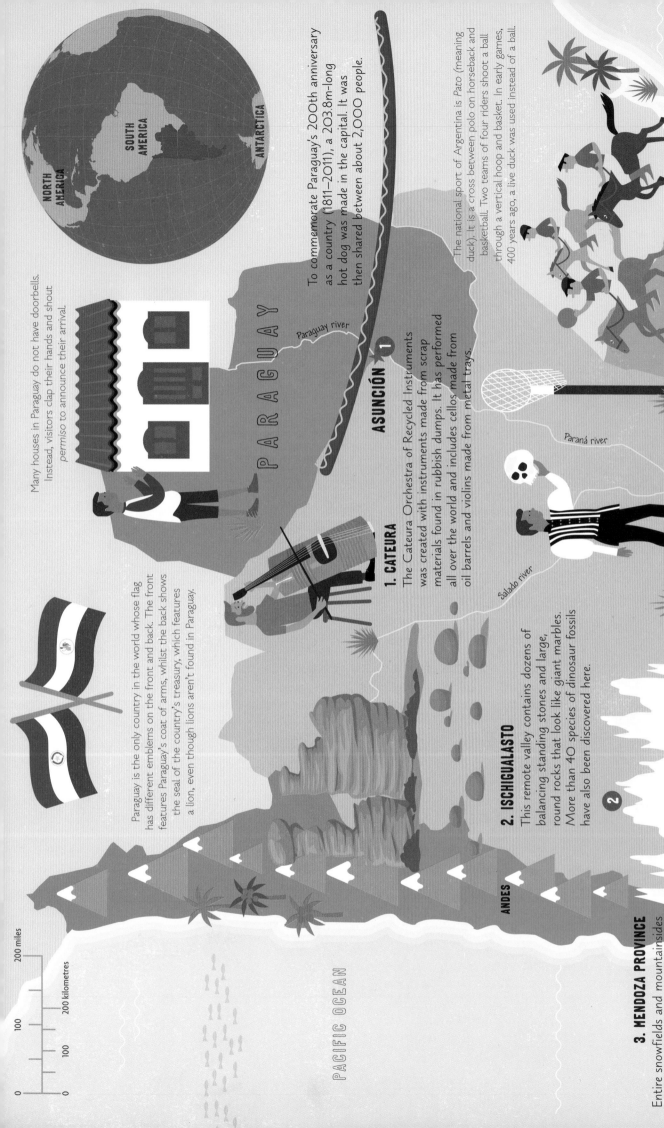

NORTH AMERICA

SOUTH AMERICA

ANTARCTICA

To commemorate Paraguay's 200th anniversary as a country (1811–2011), a 203.8m-long hot dog was made in the capital. It was then shared between about 2,000 people.

The national sport of Argentina is Pato (meaning duck). It is a cross between polo on horseback and basketball. Two teams of four riders shoot a ball through a vertical hoop and basket. In early games, 400 years ago, a live duck was used instead of a ball.

Uruguay has the world's longest national anthem. It is made up of 11 verses and 105 bars of music, that take about five minutes to play.

Many houses in Paraguay do not have doorbells. Instead, visitors clap their hands and shout *permiso* to announce their arrival.

PARAGUAY

Paraguay river

ASUNCIÓN ★ 1

1. CATEURA
The Cateura Orchestra of Recycled Instruments was created with instruments made from scrap materials found in rubbish dumps. It has performed all over the world and includes cellos made from oil barrels and violins made from metal trays.

Paraguay is the only country in the world whose flag has different emblems on the front and back. The front features Paraguay's coat of arms, whilst the back shows the seal of the country's treasury, which features a lion, even though lions aren't found in Paraguay.

Paraná river

URUGUAY

MONTEVIDEO ★ 6

6. PUNTA DEL ESTE
The fingertips of a giant hand rises from the sand of Playa Brava beach, in Uruguay. Chilean artist Mario Irrazábal created the sculpture in 1982.

ANDES

2. ISCHIGUALASTO
This remote valley contains dozens of balancing standing stones and large, round rocks that look like giant marbles. More than 40 species of dinosaur fossils have also been discovered here.

Salado river

The Teatro Dramático theatre, in Buenos Aires, received 200,000 pesos in 1955 from the will of a local man, Juan Potomachi. All they had to do in return was to use his skull during performances of *Hamlet*.

BUENOS AIRES ★ 5

2

3

3. MENDOZA PROVINCE
Entire snowfields and mountainsides are covered in blades and spikes of snow and ice in this region. These are called *penitentes* and some can reach up to 5m in height.

SANTIAGO ★

4

4. MAIPO VOLCANO
The waters of Laguna del Diamante, which were formed by a volcano, are deadly. They contain high levels of arsenic and sulphur, yet tiny bacteria and flamingos thrive here.

PACIFIC OCEAN

0 100 200 miles
0 100 200 kilometres

5. QUILMES

Tito Ingenieri spent 20 years building his house using six million glass bottles.

SOUTHERN SOUTH AMERICA

Southern South America contains four nations (Chile, Argentina, Paraguay and Uruguay) with about 71 million people combined. Most of these people live in large towns and cities leaving vast areas sparsely populated. The region contains great extremes in scenery, from the rainless deserts of northern Chile to the giant grassy plains (known as the pampas) in central Argentina and the icy wastes and islands in southern Argentina.

ATLANTIC OCEAN

With an area of about **2,780,400KM²**, Argentina is the second largest South American nation. Uruguay (**176,215KM²**) would fit more than **15 TIMES** inside Argentina. Paraguay (**406,752KM²**) is less than one-sixth of the size of Argentina.

A R G E N T I N A

Negro river

The first World Cup Final took place in 1930 in Montevideo, Uruguay, and finalists Uruguay and Argentina squabbled over whose ball to use. So they used Argentina's ball for the first half and Uruguay's ball for the second half. Uruguay won 4–2 in a match refereed by a Belgian wearing jodhpurs, a suit jacket, a tie and a flat cap.

7. Y WLADFA

A Welsh-speaking community has existed here since 1865, when settlers from Wales first arrived and stayed.

STANLEY ★
F A L K L A N D
I S L A N D S

The Argentinean publisher Eterna Cadencia has published books printed with special ink that fades away 60 days after the book is first opened. The disappearing ink in *The Book That Can't Wait* encourages people to read it quickly.

CHILE

ANDES

PACIFIC
OCEAN

1. MOUNT CHIMBORAZO

Baltazar Ushca is one of the last *hielero* or icemen in Ecuador. He hikes up close to the top of Ecuador's highest point (6,268m) to mine ice. He carries large ice blocks, weighing 20–30kg, down the mountain slopes by mule and sells them at the market in the city of Riobamba.

QUITO ★

E C U A D O R

①

The club-winged manakin is the only known bird to sing with its wings. Found in Ecuador's forests, the bird vibrates its wings to create a violin-like sound to attract a mate.

② 2. CUENCA

When Cuenca resident Jefferson Perez won his country's first ever Olympic gold medal in racewalking at the 1996 games, he received a lifetime's supply of free yoghurt as a reward.

P E R U

GALÁPAGOS ISLANDS (PART OF ECUADOR)

PACIFIC OCEAN

vampire finch

blue-footed booby

Isolated from the rest of the world for centuries, creatures have evolved here that are not found anywhere else in the world. These include some of the most northerly travelling penguins and the vampire finch, which sometimes pecks the skin and feeds on the blood of other birds.

0	50	100 miles

0	50	100 kilometres

Galápagos penguin

A small street restaurant in Peru's capital city, Lima, sells frog juice drinks to customers. Around 80 drinks are bought each day, mostly in the morning, as customers believe that the juice gives them energy for the day.

Most centipedes are tiny but the Galápagos giant centipede is a whopper. It measures over 40cm long and feasts on lizards and mice.

Although Sally Lightfoot crabs can be found along the Pacific coast of the Americas, the ones in the Galápagos Islands have an unusual trait – they are often seen cleaning ticks from the skin of marine iguanas.

Marañón river

LIMA ★

4. NAZCA

Etched into the Nazca desert are thousands of lines making up many giant patterns and drawings. These artworks are between 1,500–2,500 years old and can only be viewed fully from the air.

④

PACIFIC OCEAN

The world's longest mountain range, the Andes, runs through seven South American countries, including Ecuador, Peru and Bolivia. Out of these countries, Peru contains the most people (31.15 million people) and Bolivia the least (11.4 million).

6. TAQUILE ISLAND, LAKE TITICACA

The community of less than 2,300 people who live on this island are renowned for their artistic knitted hats and clothing. Everything is knitted by men – they are taught to knit from the age of eight.

0	100	200 miles

0	100	200 kilometres

Lying on the western side of South America, Bolivia, Ecuador and Peru all feature mountainous regions and high plains. Peru and Ecuador both have Pacific Ocean coastlines. At about 285m above sea level, Quito, in Ecuador, is the highest official capital city in the world.

...osalía Arteaga Serrano became ...cuador's first female president ...1997 . . . for just two days. The ...ader of congress, Fabián Alarcón, ...ook over as the country's leader ...wo days later.

3. NEAR CUSCO
Sacsayhuamán is a walled fortress containing giant stones, some weighing more than 20 elephants — yet it was constructed without horses for pulling the stones, cement for binding them together or even metal tools. The giant stones fit so well together that you cannot even slip a piece of paper through most of their joints.

AMAZON RAINFOREST

5. APURÍMAC CANYON
Keshwa chaca, the last remaining bridge from the time of the Incas, is rebuilt every year by local people weaving blades of grass together. Bound to tree stumps at each end, the bridge carries one person at a time, a dizzying 70m above the fast-flowing Apurímac river.

8. MADIDI NATIONAL PARK
In 2005, the right to name a new species of Madidi titi monkey discovered in this park was put up for auction. An online casino paid US$650,000 and named it in Latin after their company — *Callicebus aureipalatii* (monkey of the golden palace).

ANDES

③
⑤

BOLIVIA

⑧

7. LAKE TITICACA
The Uros peoples live on this lake on floating islands that they have made out of lake reeds woven together. The floating platforms are anchored to the bottom of the lake and have huts and houses built on top of them.

⑥ ⑦
LA PAZ ★

Every 9 November, in La Paz, people display skulls of family members. The skulls are decorated with flower petals, are offered sweets and cigarettes, and are played music to by street musicians. The day is called *Dia de los Natitas* (Day of the Skulls).

SUCRE ★ ⑨

⑩

10. UYUNI
The world's largest salt flats are about 10,582km², making them bigger than Jamaica! The Salar de Uyuni are so flat that when a little water covers their surface, they form the world's largest mirror.

9. NEAR SUCRE
Workers in a cement quarry in 1994 discovered the biggest collection of dinosaur footprints in the world. Over 5,000 dinosaur tracks were found embedded in a rockface at an almost upright angle.

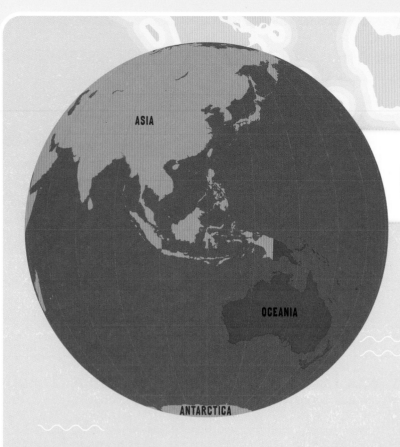

ASIA

OCEANIA

ANTARCTICA

OCEANIA

TIMOR SEA

AUSTRALIA

INDIAN
OCEAN

GREAT
AUSTRALIAN
BIGHT

Oceania consists of one giant land mass (Australia), a small number of big islands, including Papua New Guinea and New Zealand, and thousands of small islands dotted across the Pacific Ocean. Australia is huge – at 7,692km² it makes up around 5% of all the world's land. Due to the great stretches of ocean that lie between land in Oceania, many creatures have evolved that are unlike those found elsewhere in the world. These include the flightless kiwi bird in New Zealand and the kangaroo, wallaby and koala in Australia.

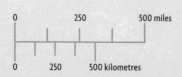

0   250   500 miles

0   250   500 kilometres

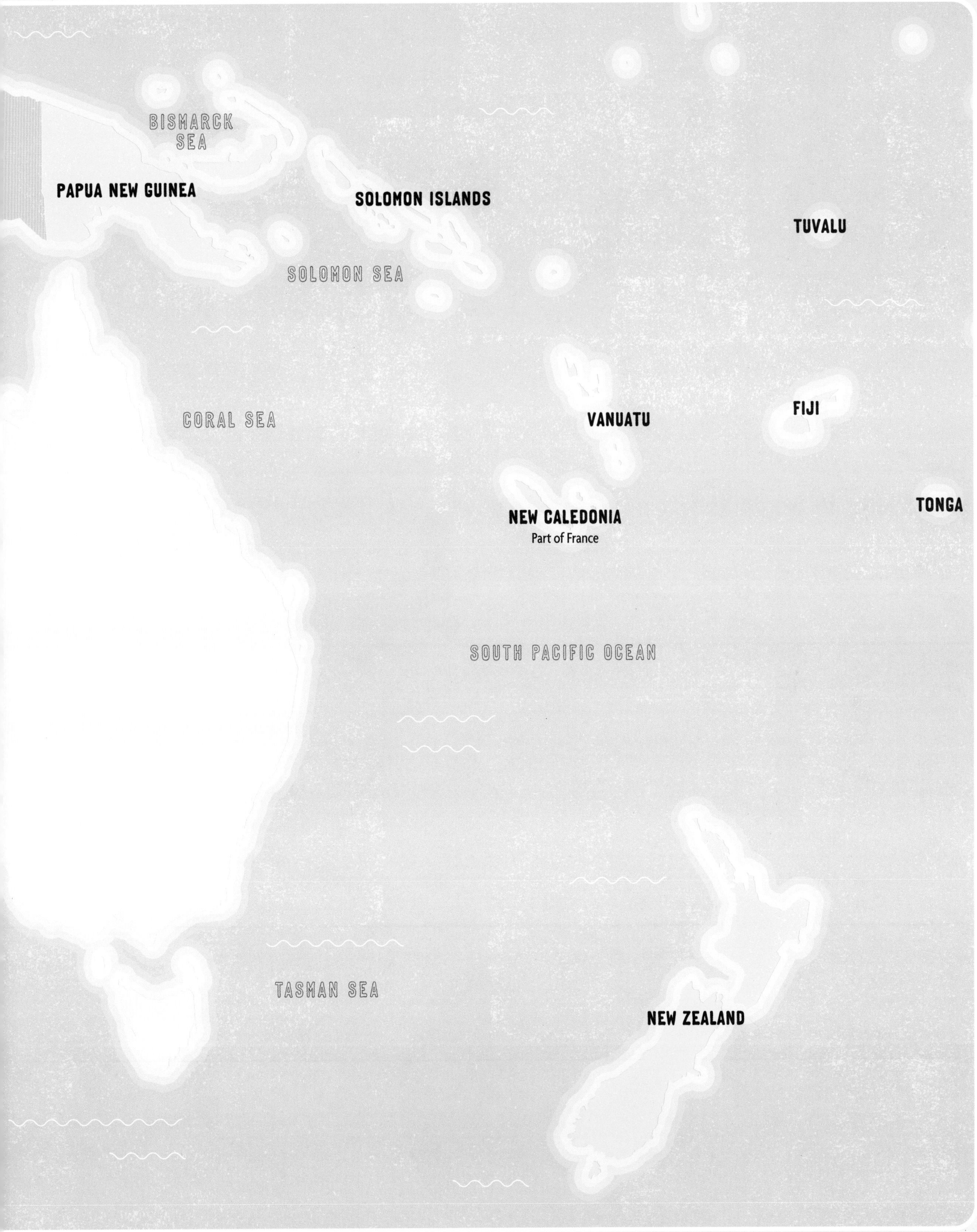

BISMARCK
SEA

PAPUA NEW GUINEA

SOLOMON ISLANDS

TUVALU

SOLOMON SEA

CORAL SEA

VANUATU

FIJI

NEW CALEDONIA
Part of France

TONGA

SOUTH PACIFIC OCEAN

TASMAN SEA

NEW ZEALAND

PAPUA NEW GUINEA

1. ANGORAM DISTRICT

In the Alamblak language spoken here, there are only words for the numbers 1, 2, 5 and 20. All other numbers are created from combinations of those four.

PAPUA NEW GUINEA

★ PORT MORESBY

2. MOUNT BOSAVI

A 2009 expedition to this remote extinct volcano uncovered more than 40 new species, including frogs with fangs in their mouths, a fish that makes grunting noises and the Bosavi woolly rat, a giant rat that weighs 1.5kg and is over 80cm long.

3. DARWIN

Every Australian winter (July or August) since 1974, a regatta in this city has featured sailboats made only from empty drinks cans.

TIMOR SEA

Wombats leave cube-shaped poos. They don't roll off logs or rocks where they are deposited. so wombats use them to mark out their territory.

```
0        250        500 miles
|----|----|----|----|----|
0        250     500 kilometres
```

INDIAN OCEAN

AUSTRALIA AND PAPUA NEW GUINEA

Australia is the sixth largest country in the world. One of its six states, Queensland, has an area of 1,730,648km^2, which is almost five times larger than Germany. The landmass was first settled by peoples from Southeast Asia over 40,000 years ago. The first European settlement was founded on the banks of Sydney Harbour in 1788. Papua New Guinea was once governed by Australia but became fully independent in 1975 and is a country of great diversity. Over 800 different languages are still spoken there by its 7.4 million people.

A duck-billed platypus has the beak and webbed feet of a duck, the smooth skin of a mole and a tail like an otter. It is one of the few mammals that produces venom from poisonous spurs on its back legs.

A U S T

4. COOBER PEDY

Most of this town's 3,500 inhabitants live underground in caves and chambers bored into the rock to protect them from the severe heat on the surface. Underground you can shop, stay in a hotel and worship at a church.

Scott Loxley walked 15,000km around Australia dressed as a Stormtrooper from the Star Wars movies to raise money for the Monash Children's Hospital. He wore out 30 pairs of shoes on his epic trek, but had just one Stormtrooper suit!

```
0        250        500 miles
|----|----|----|----|----|
0        250     500 kilometres
```

5. ESPERANCE

When parts of the Skylab space station fell to Earth and crashed into this town in 1979, the town fined US space agency NASA 400 Australian dollars for littering! The fine remained unpaid until an American radio station sent a cheque 30 years later.

Almost two-thirds of the region's **38 MILLION** population are found in Australia. Australia has over **500 NATIONAL PARKS** and more than **2,700** conservation areas.

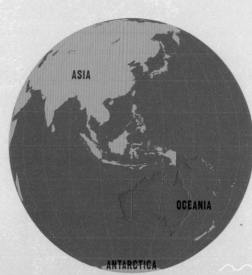

ASIA

OCEANIA

ANTARCTICA

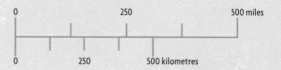

14. GULF OF CARPENTARIA

The Burke and Wills expedition consisted of a group of 19 explorers who attempted to cross Australia from south to north in 1860. They set out from Melbourne on horses and camels, with over 20 tonnes of equipment — including a bathtub, a Chinese dinner gong and dandruff combs. They managed to reach the Gulf of Carpentaria, but one person died.

GULF OF CARPENTARIA

The explorers carried 180kg of bacon and around 270 litres of rum for the camels.

CORAL SEA

13. GREAT BARRIER REEF

This is the world's largest coral reef. It even has its own floating postbox, 72km from Australia's coast in Agincourt Reef. Letters posted here get their own special Barrier Reef postmark.

15. ALICE SPRINGS

The Henley-on-Todd Regatta boat races are held here every year despite the fact there is no water to sail on. 'Sailors' instead run around the course, which is marked out on a dried-up riverbed, carrying their bottomless boats with them. It has been held every year since 1962 — except in 1993 when it was cancelled due to flooding!

12. CAIRNS

In 2015, researchers at James Cook University fitted radios to the backs of 960 bees. These radio transmitters can be tracked so that scientists can learn more about bees and how and where they travel.

11. GOLD COAST

Mice have been trained to surf on mini surfboards and ride tiny skateboards by Shane Willmott, who has even built a mouse-sized skatepark in his own garden for his pets.

Coober Pedy's golf course contains no grass, just sand and rock. Golfers carry a piece of artificial turf with them to hit the ball off.

COME AND BROWSE UNDERGROUND

KEEP OFF THE GRASS

6. FINNIS SPRINGS

A pilot discovered a drawing on the ground in 1998. Named Marree Man, it shows a 4.2km-tall aboriginal man hunting with a boomerang. To this day, no one is certain who produced it.

In 1838 it became illegal to swim at public beaches in New South Wales during the day time. This remained a law until 1902.

10. SYDNEY

Australia's first police force, called the Night Watch, was made up of a dozen convicted criminals. They were selected in 1789 by Captain Arthur Phillip, the first governor of Australia.

★ CANBERRA

In 2012, Rob Ginnivan ran a half marathon (21.1km) in 2 hours, 18 minutes in a hot air balloon flying above Canberra. He completed his feat running on a treadmill in the balloon's basket.

7. PORT ADELAIDE

In 2000, Australia, not North Africa or the Middle East, had the most wild camels in the world with numbers rising above one million. The very first camel in Australia was called Harry and arrived in Adelaide in 1840. Today there are about 300,000 wild camels in Australia.

8. MELBOURNE

Melbourne was originally called Batmania. It was nothing to do with the comic book superhero but rather, it was named after John Batman who explored the area in 1835.

TASMAN SEA

9. TASMANIA

In the 1830s, 300 female convicts in Hobart all lifted their skirts and bared their bottoms during a chapel service at the governor of Tasmania in protest at their working conditions.

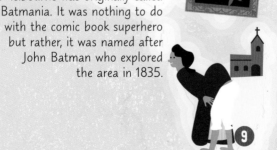

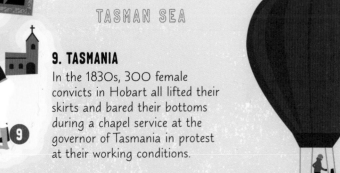

NEW ZEALAND

Scattered across the mighty Pacific Ocean lie thousands and thousands of islands, many of which are the result of volcanic activity. New Zealand's North and South Islands are the largest, with a total area of 268,107km² and over 4.6 million inhabitants.

1. AUCKLAND

Porter and Monty are two dogs with a difference. They were taught to drive a car by an animal rescue charity in 2012. Both dogs can drive a modified Mini: the dogs' legs can reach the accelerator and brake pedals, whilst their front paws turn the steering wheel.

2. CAMBRIDGE

Dairy farmer and tree enthusiast, Barry Cox grew a church out of living trees between 2011 and 2015. He trained trees around an iron frame to create a roof made of cut-leaf alder and walls made of Australian tea trees. The church is now open for couples looking for a leafy place to get married.

3. WAITOMO

You don't need a torch inside Waitomo Caves, even though they're deep and dark, as they are lit up by thousands of tiny glow-worms. These creatures give out an eerie blue light from their tails, which attracts small insects towards them to eat. Glow-worms are actually beetles, and this one – *Arachnocampa luminosa* – is found only in New Zealand.

4. TAUMATA HILL

The longest place name in New Zealand is Taumata whakatangi hangakoauau o tamatea turi pukakapiki maunga horo nuku pokai whenua kitanatahu! Translated, this means, 'the place where Tamatea [a local chief], the man with the big knees, who slid, climbed and swallowed mountains, known as "landeater", played his flute to his loved one.'

TAUMATA WHAKATANGI HANGAKOAUAU O TAMATEA TURI PUKAKAPIKI MAUNGA HORO NUKU POKAI WHENUA KITANATAHU

5. KAHURANGI NATIONAL PARK

In the past 25 years, only two milky-white albino *Powelliphanta* snails have been spotted. These giant snails have shells up to 9cm in diameter and are carnivorous, voraciously gobbling up slugs and earthworms.

In 1990, long before *Lord of the Rings* was filmed in New Zealand, the country's Prime Minister appointed Ian Brackenbury Channell as the official Wizard of New Zealand. His official tasks include to 'bless new enterprises, cheer up the population and attract tourists.'

6. WESTLAND NATIONAL PARK

There's an icy glacier, called Franz Josef, right in the middle of a tropical forest here. The 12km-long glacier sometimes flows at a rate of 70cm per day.

7. QUEENSTOWN

During the winter festival here, competitors compete with dogs in barking competitions, slide down snowy hills on suitcases or race round an obstacle course that includes a dip in chilly Lake Wakatipu in just their underwear.

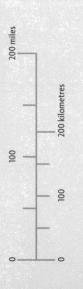

8. DUNEDIN

This picturesque town is home to the 350m-long Baldwin Street, the world's steepest town road. For every 2.8m you travel along the street, you climb 1m. Since 1988, the Baldwin Street Gutbuster – a gruelling running race to the top of the street and down again – has been held here.

NORTH ISLAND

SOUTH ISLAND

NEW ZEALAND

★ WELLINGTON

TASMAN SEA

PACIFIC OCEAN

200 miles

200 kilometres

0   100   200

0   100   200

ASIA

OCEANIA

ANTARCTICA

THE PACIFIC ISLANDS

The Pacific Ocean covers one-third of Earth's surface, making it the world's largest and deepest ocean. Within it are over 25,000 islands (more than there are in all of the rest of the oceans combined), yet only about 5,000 of these islands are inhabited.

ASIA

OCEANIA

ANTARCTICA

9. YAP

Until the early 20th century, people on this island used large circular limestone stones, called Rai, for money. Some were as big as 4m wide. Fortunately, people left the larger stones where they were and just swapped ownership by word of mouth.

10. EIL MALK

This small island contains Jellyfish Lake, which is packed full of millions of golden jellyfish whose sting has been weakened over generations so that people can swim with them. The jellyfish migrate across the lake, following the sun, every day.

11. NEAR PALAU

In 1944, American submarine USS Tullibee sank itself accidentally. It fired two torpedoes at an enemy ship, but one of them travelled in a circle and hit the sub, causing it to sink.

12. SANDY ISLAND

In 1876, Sandy Island was reported by a whaling ship and placed on maps and charts. However, in 2012, a survey ship sailed to its location and discovered it wasn't there. It was then struck off the world's maps.

13. VANUATU

One of the post offices here is located 3m underwater. A special float is placed on the sea's surface when the office is open. People use waterproof postcards and stamps, and dive down to use the post office.

14. VITU LEVU

In Fiji the top of the head is sacred and shouldn't be touched by another person. When Christian missionary Thomas Baker touched the head of a local chieftain in 1867, he was killed. Part of his remaining shoe is displayed in the Fiji Museum, Suva.

15. APIA

The first ever rugby match between Fiji and Samoa kicked off in Apia, Samoa's capital, in 1924 at 7am so that the players could go to work afterwards. The game took place on a pitch that had a palm tree growing out of the middle. Fiji were the winners!

16. APIA

In 1955, the MV Joyita set off from Apia, bound for the Tokelau Islands, 48 hours away. However, it never arrived. Five weeks later, and without any radio calls or distress signals in between, the ship was found floating near Fiji, without its 25-person crew. To this day, no one knows what turned it into a ghost ship.

17. TEAHUPO'O

In 2015, a man surfed giant ocean waves in Tahiti riding his motorbike. Robbie Maddison's KTM 250 SX motorbike was fitted with water skis and a special flotation air bag for the challenge.

18. RAPA NUI (EASTER ISLAND)

This island is over 2,000km away from other inhabited lands, yet the people on it sculpted almost 900 fearsome stone statues, called moai, out of volcanic rock without any metal tools, between approximately 1200 and 1600ce. The largest of the statues is 9m tall and weighs over 74 tonnes.

MICRONESIA

NORTHERN MARIANA (USA)

GUAM (USA)

PALAU

PAPUA NEW GUINEA

PORT MORESBY ★

In Fiji, a man wishing to marry is expected to bring his soon-to-be father-in-law a present of a whale tooth. This is known as a tabua.

SOLOMON ISLANDS

NEW CALEDONIA (FRANCE)

VANUATU

MARSHALL ISLANDS

KIRIBATI

NAURU

PACIFIC OCEAN

TUVALU

SAMOA

AMERICAN SAMOA

FIJI

TONGA

NIUE

HAWAII (USA)

COOK ISLANDS

FRENCH POLYNESIA

RAPA NUI (EASTER ISLAND)

0   250   500 miles
0   250   500 kilometres

THE ARCTIC AND GREENLAND

The Arctic Circle contains Earth's most northerly land, ice and water. It includes the northernmost parts of Canada, Russia and Scandinavia, as well as most of Greenland — the world's biggest island. Most of Greenland's 56,000 people live along its 44,0987km coast in small settlements. Only five of these have over 3,000 inhabitants.

Greenland is a self-governing province of Denmark but it nearly became part of the United States. In 1946, they offered to buy Greenland for US$100 million but Denmark turned the offer down.

CHUKCH SEA

BEAUFORT SEA

1. CAMP CENTURY

In 1960, the United States began building a top secret missile launch site under the ice of northern Greenland without anyone, including Greenland or Denmark, knowing. Code-named Project Iceworm, the proposed base was to include 4,000km of tunnels able to store up to 600 nuclear missiles, but plans were abandoned in 1966.

3. UUMMANNAQ

The World Ice Golf Championship has been held on an ice shelf here since 1997. Each year the course has to be reshaped with smoothed out snow for the greens. With temperatures sometimes dropping below −50°C, golfers not only have to wrap up warm, they also need to avoid using golf clubs with graphite shafts as these can shatter in such low temperatures.

2. SIORAPALUK

In this most northerly village in the world, one of the traditional dishes is rotting seabirds. *Kiviaq* is sealskin stuffed with dozens of auk birds. It is left to ferment for between three and 18 months under a pile of rocks.

HUDSON BAY

4. ILULISSAT

After months of darkness, the sun returns to this northern Greenland town in January. On the 13 minute of the 13th hour on the 13 January, the schoolchildren are taken by dog sled to Holms Bakke hill to sing songs to welcome the sun back.

② ①

BAFFIN BAY

G R E E N L A N D

③

⑤④

DAVIS STRAIT

LABRADOR SEA

GREENLAND SEA

★ NUUK

Some prisoners at the Nuuk Correctional Institute, Greenland's main prison, hold the keys to their own cells! They have to be in the prison from 9.30pm until 6am the next day, but are then free to leave to visit their families or to go to work.

DENMARK STRAIT

5. QILAKITSOQ

Two local brothers discovered eight mummies here in 1972. The eight bodies had been freeze-dried by the cold climate so were well preserved, even though they had all died around 1475 — almost 500 years earlier.

ATLANTIC OCEAN

EAST
SIBERIAN SEA

Arctic terns in Greenland are frequent fliers. They rack up the air miles by flying south to Antarctica and back to the Arctic each year, averaging around 70,000km – the longest migration of any animal.

NORTH
AMERICA

SOUTH
AMERICA

The narwhal is called 'the unicorn of the sea' due to a gigantic tusk that can grow to over 3m long. The spear isn't for catching fish, though – instead it is used as a water sensor to detect tiny changes in temperature and chemicals in the seawater to seek out prey.

LAPTEV
SEA

In certain conditions, ice crystals freezing in air that is colder than the ocean water can form expanses of beautiful frost flowers across the Arctic waters.

At **2,166,086KM²**, Greenland is the world's largest island. Its only national park measures **972,000KM²**, making it bigger than more than **160** of the world's countries. There are **0** roads between Greenland's settlements. All inter-town travel is by sea or from one of its **15** airports.

ARCTIC OCEAN

NORTH POLE

On the floor of the Arctic Ocean, about 4,261m below sea level, is a Russian flag. It was put there in 2007 by a small Russian submarine as they wanted to claim the North Pole as their territory. However, their claim was turned down by the United Nations.

KARA
SEA

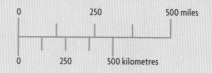

0	250	500 miles

0	250	500 kilometres

Long before you could get Wi-Fi in many towns and cities of the world, it was available near the North Pole after two Intel employees set up a Wi-Fi hotspot in 2005 at Barneo Ice Camp – a seasonal research base, just 80km from the North Pole.

New Year is celebrated twice on the same day in Greenland, once at 8pm – when it becomes New Year in Denmark – and again at midnight. On both occasions, many rockets and fireworks are fired in celebration.

BARENTS SEA

British swimmer, Lewis Gordon Pugh, once swam for almost 19 minutes in the incredibly cold water surrounding the North Pole . . . without a wetsuit on!

The North Pole is totally dark from the end of October until the end of January. The sun actually disappears over the horizon in late September but twilight exists for a month. After that, you won't see the sun rise again for over 170 days.

NORWEGIAN
SEA

1. SOUTH SHETLAND ISLANDS

In 2014, Ramón Navarro from Chile surfed the icy cold waters close to Antarctica. Brrrr!

4. JAMES ROSS ISLAND

Fossilized dinosaur remains found in Antarctica prove it hasn't always been icy here. Dinosaur fossils were first found here in 1986 and in 2011, a titanosaur bone was discovered on James Ross Island.

WEDDELL SEA

ATLANTIC OCEAN

2. CARLINI STATION

Metallica became the first major rock band to play a concert in Antarctica. This 2013 gig at the Argentinian research base also meant that they were the first band to do a concert on all seven of Earth's continents.

3. ESPERANZA BASE, HOPE BAY

In 1978, the first Antarctica baby was born, and named Emilio Marcos Palma. His mother had been flown out by the Argentinian government months earlier so they could claim that he was Antarctica's only true citizen!

6. WEDDELL SEA

In 1904, Gilbert Kerr, a member of the Scottish Antarctic Expedition of 1902–04, played tunes on his bagpipes to emperor penguins — Antarctica's first live concert!

BELLINGSHAUSEN SEA

A N T A R

7. UNION GLACIER, BASE OF ELLSWORTH MOUNTAINS

The Antarctic Ice Marathon is held here every year. Runners are flown in by private jet from Argentina to take part. The fastest time to complete the 42.2km race is 3 hours, 34 minutes.

8. BAY OF WHALES

The Antarctic Snow Cruiser was a giant 17m-long truck with an aircraft on its roof that was used here in the 1940s. The vehicle was lost under the snow, found in 1958, and then lost again!

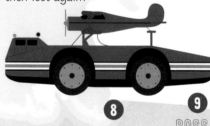

5. GOUDIER ISLAND

This tiny, rocky outcrop is a British base and is home to a post office. The post office manager has to live without phone, internet, central heating and running water, and work alongside 2,000 penguins. Despite the tough conditions, almost 1,000 people applied for the job in 2015.

AMUNDSEN SEA

The truck wasn't good at gripping ice when moving forward, so its longest journey of 148km was made in reverse.

ROSS SE

Larger than Europe, but with no more than 5,000 people there at any one time, Antarctica was the last continent to be discovered. The temperature of this icy desert is usually below –20°C, but –89.2°C was recorded at Vostok Station in 1983. But however cold it gets here, Deep Lake never freezes because it is so salty.

PACIFIC OCEAN

B-15

ANTARCTICA

9. ROSS ICE SHELF

One of the largest icebergs (named B-15) broke free from this ice shelf in 2000. At 11,000km², it's half the size of Wales!

0   15   30 miles

0   15   30 kilometres

In winter, the sea ice around Antarctica grows. It adds up to 30,000km^2 to the continent's area each day — this extra area is almost the size of Belgium.

SOUTH AMERICA

INDIAN OCEAN

14. SOUTH POLE

Roald Amundsen led the first expedition to reach the South Pole in 1911 on foot and using dog sleds. UK television presenter Helen Skelton used a snow kite to pull her along on skis and also cycled 167km over snow and ice on a special bike to reach the South Pole 101 years later.

15. DAVIS STATION

Antarctica's sculpture garden doesn't contain any plants, but it does have plenty of penguins and a few sculptures. The oldest sculpture is Fred the Head, carved out of wood by a plumber in 1977.

15

C T I C A

13. AMUNDSEN-SCOTT SOUTH POLE STATION

In 1985, Randall Chambers and Patricia Manglicmot had their wedding at this research base.

DAVIS SEA

The cold waters around Antarctica are rich in krill (small shrimp-like creatures) — a blue whale's favourite food. An adult blue whale can eat 3,600kg of krill each day!

VOSTOK STATION ●

12. TAYLOR VALLEY

Water coloured red by iron oxides flows from the edge of a glacier into West Lake Bonney. Discovered in 1911, it has been given the gruesome name of Blood Falls.

Inside, preserved by the cold climate, are more than 8,000 items from the expedition, including tins of baked beans and bottles of tomato ketchup.

10. CAPE EVANS, ROSS ISLAND

The hut Captain Scott and his team used as a base on their 1911–12 expedition to reach the South Pole still stands. It is made of wood and insulated with seaweed.

DEEP LAKE ●
 12

 10   11

Around **61%** of Earth's fresh water is locked up in Antarctica's ice, which in places is a staggering **5.5KM DEEP**. If all of Antarctica's ice melted, then the world's seas and oceans would rise by **50–65M**.

11. McMURDO STATION

This base contains Antarctica's only cash machines. They dispense US dollars to visitors and workers.

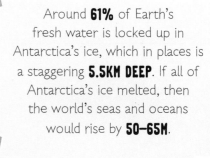

MORE ODDITIES

When it comes to oddities around the world, this book is just the beginning. There's lots, lots more to explore and discover. Here are some extra oddities for you to enjoy. And after you've read these, why not become an oddity explorer yourself? You can visit odd and fascinating places in your local area or head off on a virtual journey using books and the internet to find your own.

KAGOSHIMA, JAPAN

Keen gardener Manabu Oono grew the world's heaviest radish in 2003. It had a circumference of 119cm and weighed a hefty 31.1kg!

SVENDBORG, DENMARK

Each year in May, practical jokers and circus funnymen meet at the International Clown Festival. Some of the clowns visit hospitals and schools in the region to bring some cheer.

LOS ANGELES, USA

Jay Ohrberg's American Dream was a stretched limo car. It measured a staggering 30.5m long, had 26 wheels and included a hot tub and a helicopter landing pad.

OKLAHOMA, USA

The World Championship Cow Chip Throw occurs in the town of Beaver every April. A cow chip is a dried piece of cow poo!

SARDINIA

Casu Marzu is a local delicacy in Sardinia and is still made, even though it is against the law. It features rancid sheep milk infested with maggots, which is eaten whilst the maggots remain alive in the cheese.

ULAANBAATAR, MONGOLIA

The Mongolian Stock Exchange is the world's smallest by the size of market. It opened in 1991 and is inside a former children's cinema!

BRAZIL

Brazil couldn't afford to send its athletes to the 1932 Los Angeles Olympics so its competitors travelled there on a cargo ship and sold coffee on the way to fund their trip. And because the Port of Los Angeles charged US$1 for everyone who got off a ship there, athletes who were thought to be unlikely to win Olympic medals were forced to stay onboard.

YANGJU, SOUTH KOREA

The largest cup of coffee in the world was brewed by Caffe Bene in 2014. The giant mug held 14,228.1 litres of coffee — enough to fill around 40,000 average-sized mugs!

NO CATS ALLOWED

LONGYEARBYEN, ON THE ISLAND OF SVALBARD, NORWAY

In Longyearbyen, the world's most northerly town, it is illegal to keep a pet cat because they hunt the birds.

CHICHÉN ITZA, MEXICO

El Castillo is a massive pyramid built by the ancient Maya during the 11th and 13th centuries. There are 365 steps — one for each day of the year. It's positioned so that, twice a year, a shadow seems to slide down the steps like a snake when the sun sets!

WHERE IN THE WORLD?

So you think you know all about the odd things dotted around our planet? Why not take this global challenge to recall the locations of some of the strange sights, curious creatures, and odd events and places you've discovered in the book. If you can get more than half of the questions correct, without peeking at the answers at the bottom of the right-hand page, then you are an *Atlas of Oddities* Champ!

1. Which chilly continent is home to Blood Falls?

2. Which North African country should you visit to see goats in argan trees?

3. Which Indian city is home to the haunted fort of Bhangarh?

4. In which US state is it illegal to go fishing whilst on the back of a giraffe?

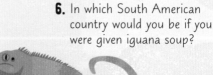

5. Where in eastern Asia is the International Friendship Exhibition?

6. In which South American country would you be if you were given iguana soup?

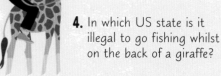

7. Where in China was the first goldfish beauty pageant held?

8. Which South African country has an underground lake with golden cave catfish in?

9. Where in New Zealand can you ride down a hill on a suitcase and have a dip in a chilly lake in your underwear?

10. Which European country is home to the Worm Charming World Championships?

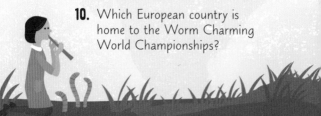

11. Where in Scandinavia is the Grandmothers Festival held?

12. Which South American city has a monkey sculpture made from flip-flops in one of its parks?

13. In which North American country can you see the world's largest sausage statue?

14. Which US city is home to the Museum of Bad Art?

15. Where in eastern Africa are camels used to deliver library books?

16. Where in western Africa was the SuperCroc fossil found?

17. Where in Australia did Shane Willmott build a mouse-sized skatepark?

18. In which country can you take part in a cucumber festival?

19. Which south American country commemorated its 200th anniversary as a country by making a giant hot dog?

20. Where in Europe is the Frog Museum?

21. Which Spanish town holds a massive tomato fight, called La Tomatina, each year?

22. Where would you be if you were visiting the Kawah Ijen volcano, whose lava is electric blue at night?

ANSWERS: 1. Antarctica 2. Morocco 3. Rajasthan 4. Idaho 5. North Korea 6. French Guiana 7. Fuzhou 8. Namibia 9. Queenstown 10. England 11. Bodø, Norway 12. Sao Paulo, Brazil 13. Canada 14. Boston, Massachusetts 15. Garissa, Kenya 16. Gadoufaoua, Niger 17. Gold Coast 18. Russia 19. Paraguay 20. Estavery-le-Lac, Switzerland 21. Buñol 22. Indonesia

89

INDEX